KU-736-445

Missing Being Mrs

"Wow... Jen allows us right inside her heart. She shares exactly how it feels when an apparently happy, successful marriage abruptly ends... She writes so well there was no putting the book down until it was finished."
– **Jennifer Rees Larcombe**

"I read this book in one sitting... It will be very strengthening and encouraging to so many in similar situations."
– **Celia Bowring,** CARE

ACC. No: **03246353**

Missing
Being Mrs

Surviving divorce
without losing
your friends, your faith,
or your mind

Jennifer Croly

MONARCH
BOOKS

Oxford, UK & Grand Rapids, Michigan, USA

Text copyright © 2004 Jennifer Croly
This edition copyright © 2015 Lion Hudson

The right of Jennifer Croly to be identified as the author of this work has been asserted by him in accordance with the Copyright, Designs and Patents Act 1988.

All rights reserved. No part of this publication may be reproduced or transmitted in any form or by any means, electronic or mechanical, including photocopy, recording, or any information storage and retrieval system, without permission in writing from the publisher.

Published by Monarch Books
an imprint of
Lion Hudson plc
Wilkinson House, Jordan Hill Road,
Oxford OX2 8DR, England
Email: monarch@lionhudson.com
www.lionhudson.com/monarch

ISBN 978 0 85721 639 7
e-ISBN 978 0 85721 640 3

First edition 2004
This edition 2015

Acknowledgments
Unless otherwise stated, Scripture quotations are taken from
The Message by Eugene H. Peterson, © 2002 by NavPress.
Used by permission of NavPress. All rights reserved.

A catalogue record for this book is available from the British Library

Printed and bound in the UK, April 2015, LH26

Contents

DEDICATION

This book is dedicated to Jan Greenough.
Without her support and endless cups of weak Earl Grey
it would never have been written.

Chapter 1

Have They Really Gone?

The nightmare begins

I have trouble watching people walk out of doors. Just ordinary doors. Just leaving the room. I have real trouble watching people walk out of doors. Especially if I love them. I know exactly why. On 2nd September 1997 my husband and two daughters walked out of our back door. Nothing was ever the same again.

A strange reality

I lost my husband and two of my four children on the same day. They left in the morning as usual, the girls happily following their dad out of the door, and they didn't come back. At first I didn't believe it. I couldn't believe it. I couldn't conceive the reality of it in my head. Reality turned into a nightmare. That's a cliché because it's true.

I lost my husband and two children on the same day. I wanted to dial 999! I wanted to dial 911! Fire? Police? Ambulance? Coastguard? Call out the Marines? But there was no emergency service to deal with this emergency, and no one did anything about it. No one seemed to care. Worse, no one seemed to notice. It was as if it wasn't happening. There was no outcry, no newspaper headlines, no outpouring of national sympathy. My girls had been taken from me and they treated it as *normal*. What sort of nightmare was this? Nightmare acting as reality. A nightmare where you try to speak but can't be heard. My girls had gone. They'd been taken and no one did anything about it.

I went to Social Services. They looked concerned, but powerless. I went to a solicitor, who showed me his filing cabinets. "It's very common," he said. "It happens every day." It was just a job to him. "BUT SOMEONE HAS TAKEN MY CHILDREN!" My heart was screaming but my voice was level. "You may see this every day, but it's the first time it has happened to me," I tried to explain. "These are not statistics; they are my daughters, and they have been taken away from me."

"There's no law against it," he said. "It's not worth bothering the police with. It would only cause the girls more distress."

Obviously he didn't understand. I searched for a more sympathetic ear. Two more solicitors said the same thing. One recommended a counsellor. She listened for an hour and then summed up the situation neatly: "It seems to me," she said, "that you want someone to say this can't happen, but in my experience I'm very much afraid that it can."

I lost my husband and two children on the same day. At a quarter to nine. Just before I went to work. I told my boss what had happened. He looked shocked, pitying, powerless. So did everyone. No one moved. No one did anything. A force field suddenly opened up around me. People walked by giving me a six-foot clearance. It was as if any closer would be dangerous. My boss was at a complete loss. Totally out of his depth. "Take some time off," he said, as a drowning man clutches at a piece of passing flotsam. "Take some time off if you want – you must have some practicalities to sort out." Life moved on again. It looked like a video playing to itself.

I lost my husband and two children on the same day and I couldn't take it in. "This can't be right," my mind reasoned. "Not my husband! Not my man! Not *my* man! GOD! You can do all things! Make it right again. Bring them back to me." I prayed. I pleaded. I couldn't believe it. Soon they'd all come walking in again. I'd hear the car on the gravel and their voices ringing as they jostled in at the door. Laden with packages, home from the shops, look at the money they'd made Daddy spend again! Twisting him round their little fingers. That's girls for you. Ten and twelve they were, a vulnerable age. They couldn't have gone. That only happens in nightmares.

I lost my husband and two of my children on the same day. "Well at least you still have the boys," someone said. I think that was meant to be comforting. My mind flipped to the memory of their young faces when they were told. So many emotions in one moment. The shock, the total disbelief, the grief. Trying to make sense of it all. They were sharing the same nightmare. Trying to be strong. Trying to be strong for *me*. But that was all the wrong way round! I should be strong for them. What sort of reality was this? Yes, I still had the boys. We were now a family of three, not six. I kept cooking too much food. There was suddenly too much space in the house. It was unnaturally quiet. Empty bedrooms. I shut the doors. Empty spaces at the table – we tried to ignore them. We carried on, attempting to be normal. Remind me, what *was* normal?

On that day I had lost him for ever, but my head expected him to walk in the door again, smiling, familiar, normal, like he had every day of my adult life. Soon I would wake up and everything would be normal again. Soon he would walk in and laugh and say what an idiot I'd been to worry. Soon he would come to his senses and return and say sorry and we'd kiss and make up. Like we'd always done. We'd always overcome any problem together.

Now, it seemed, there was no "together". All our adult lives we'd been together. Now I was alone. I'd never been alone before. Now, everywhere I went I would go alone.

So, inexorably, the nightmare rolled on, daily played out in familiar settings. There was never any end to it. There was never any funeral. No public demonstration of mourning. No cards, no flowers, no gathering of sympathetic friends. There was no acknowledgement of our loss. No one to share past happy memories with. It was as if the past was wiped out. As if it had never existed. Twenty-two years suddenly gone. My whole adult life. My husband. Their father. Our family. Gone.

In those early days I once had a dream. It was an ordinary dream. I was walking beside him in easy familiarity and the children were all around, running backwards and forwards, shouting and complaining. A normal day out, in my dream. Reality returned to a recognised shape, feelings relaxed, happiness returned... then I woke, and the nightmare invaded with all its nightmare feelings. I woke up *into* the nightmare. "That's not right!" my heart screamed, as the mangling pains twisted somewhere very deep and the tears forced their way out of my eyes. Reality shifted again. My mind couldn't get round it. "This isn't right! You're supposed to wake up *out* of the nightmare, not into it!" The tears, temporarily staunched in dreamland, now welled up again and flowed freely in disappointment.

Reality was a dream.

The nightmare *is* reality.

I couldn't believe it.

"God! Say it's not true! Say it's not happening!"

"GOD!" I cried.

"Nothing will ever be the same again," he said, ever truthful.

"God! You can't mean that!"

"I will never leave you," he said.

I lost my husband and two children on the same day. And no one seemed to understand why I was crying. After all, people walk out of their marriages every day.

I was thrown into a strange and totally unexpected reality. In fact the whole meaning of what we call "reality" seemed to me to have changed. The impossible was suddenly my everyday experience. The unbearable was being daily borne. What sort of reality was this? How can I explain it?

Maybe you remember the day Princess Diana died, and the awful shock that accompanied that news. Wasn't it unreal? Yet to me it almost seemed quite reassuringly normal. First my husband had left, then Princess Diana died; the next day the newsreader reported that little green men had landed from Mars and when I looked out of the window in the morning the sky had turned fluorescent orange. Well, all right, the last two didn't happen, but I don't think I would have been surprised if they had. I had lost all ability to gauge what reality *was* because so much of what I had believed to be true had turned into its own opposite.

One day I was married, the next I was single. One day I was the mother of a large family milling around at home. The next I faced a new reality: single parent to two boys and parent-at-a-distance to two girls. How do you parent your children when you only see them once a week? How do you parent at all when your inner self is disintegrating? How was I ever going to get used to a reality like that?

The world I walked through in the daytime looked false and unreal, yet in my dreams all was "normal". Then I woke again to the reality of a nightmare. That was one of the most distressing experiences I had at the time. When you are in a dream, you think it is real. Then you wake up and find it's not. You really have lost the people you love most, which has to be anyone's worst nightmare.

The strangest reality of all was that the one who had been my closest friend was now acting as my worst enemy. The person I knew best in the world had turned into a stranger. The one I knew I could trust with my life I could no longer depend on at all. I really couldn't take this in. My husband was gone yet not dead, so I couldn't have a funeral, couldn't share the sad news with friends and family, and couldn't begin the process of grieving. Yet although alive he was lost to me. It was very difficult to know how to act or what to feel in this situation. It was all so bizarre. He looked like my man; he sounded like him and then he behaved totally contrarily to all I had ever known of him. Totally out of character. It was as if there was an alien in my husband's body! How could *that* be reality? That really was the sort of thing that only happens in horror movies or nightmares.

How do you deal with such a strange and distressing reality? It is hard for other people to realise what a shock it is. It is hard for them to believe that you really didn't see it coming. I didn't see it coming. Like many others before me, and many doubtless to come, I honestly thought that it would never happen to me. I was young when I married at 20, but not thoughtless. I was a committed Christian marrying a committed Christian and I believed that marriage was for life. Both sets of my grandparents had been married until death robbed them of their partner. My parents have been married for over 50 years. With such a family history I knew that marriage for life was a real possibility. There would always be problems, but I believed that there was no problem that we couldn't solve together. There was certainly no problem *God* couldn't solve, if we asked him. I believed God had put us together. The vows I took, I took in church and meant seriously. So did he. We faced all the ups and downs that life inevitably brings along together, and our relationship was strengthened. After 22 years of marriage, and four lovely children, I was very secure in the knowledge that our friendship and love would last throughout this life and beyond. I never once considered that he would leave. It just didn't seem a possibility. I would have staked my life on it.

What I didn't realise is that, although it takes two to make a marriage, it only takes one to break it. When it came to it there was no discussing of problems, no involvement of professional help, and no prayerful appeal to God. If one partner decides unilaterally to walk away from the marriage, there is nothing the other can do about it. The pain of that decision and its consequent effects on children, grandparents, friends and family is sudden and inevitable. It simply has to be endured.

I had no idea that emotional pain could be so intense, just so utterly painful. It is hard to explain. I think that because the wounds are invisible people think they are not there. In the first shock of loss, psychologists, I have since learnt, talk of "denial". Denial seems such a negative word, like a refusal to accept the facts, almost as if one *wanted* to live in a fantasy, but really it is a very helpful trick of the mind. Shock and denial are useful friends; they offer some psychological protection. The brute facts are far too painful to accept all at once and denial is a way of easing the pain. When a partner leaves, the loss is so great it is totally unbearable, but maybe it becomes bearable if you think of it as being only temporary. "He'll be back by Christmas." "She'll soon realise she can't live on her own." "He'll come to his senses eventually." "She'll realise it's all been a big mistake..." To look at any other alternative would just be too much to bear to begin with.

Friends at this stage also don't want to believe that it is true either, and they bolster you with stories of people who were separated for six months, a year, two years, ten years, until it all ended happily ever after. And of course there always is that possibility that your partner *will* come back, so for six months, a year, two years, or however long it takes, you hang on, hoping for reconciliation. Christian friends pray and quote "What God has joined together, let no man put asunder" and remind you that nothing is impossible for God. Convinced that God wants you together, they pray like they have never prayed before and alert their intercessory groups and leave your name on monastery prayer lists. Meanwhile I simply stood in shock and tried to get used to the idea of what had happened to me. I appreciated the people who stood with me. Literally hundreds of people prayed for the restoration of my marriage. I am so grateful to them for their support, love and prayers. So why didn't God answer their prayers? Why didn't God, of all people, DO something?

God never promised me he would bring my husband back. He promised to take care of me, and that he has done. He told me not to fear and he promised to strengthen me. He promised he would never leave me. Those promises he has kept.

I will never leave you nor forsake you

It's funny – people are kind and want to encourage you to hope for the best, but I found God to be much more of a realist. The day after my husband told me he was leaving, my daily readings said, "Take your share of suffering like a good soldier of Christ" (2 Timothy 2:3, Living Bible). There's nothing like not mincing your words!

A couple of days later the reading was 1 Peter 4:1–2: "So since Christ suffered in the flesh for you, arm yourself with the same thought and purpose (patiently to suffer rather than fail to please God). For whoever has suffered in the flesh is done with sin [has stopped pleasing themselves and the world and pleases God]", Amplified Bible.

Suddenly, when all else that had seemed real looked

like a stage set, like a picture of reality, the truth of what I was reading in the Bible seemed to fit with the strange new reality I was experiencing. This hurt! And God knew it! This really, really hurt and there was nothing I could do about it. This really was reality. It is not a popular subject, but the Bible consistently teaches that we will suffer. Here in the comfortable West we always seem surprised by this (although brothers and sisters in other countries know suffering as a daily reality).

A couple of days later my attention was drawn to "Stop being afraid of what you are about to suffer. Hold fast the faith even when facing death and I will give you a crown of life – an unending glorious future" (Revelation 2:10, Living Bible), and then, "These troubles and suffering of ours are, after all, quite small and won't last very long. Yet this short time of distress will result in God's richest blessing upon us for ever and ever!" (2 Corinthians 4:17, Living Bible).

Now, before we go any further, let's get one thing straight. I am absolutely sure that God has no wish to see people suffer. Nor does he bring suffering our way in order to teach us things or make us turn to him. That's a lie! God binds himself to us with love, not with pain. He himself would rather take the hurt than see us suffer, as the cross clearly demonstrates. The origin of suffering is with mankind or with the church's enemy, Satan. We suffer as the consequence of our own actions or the actions of other people. The only one to delight in our suffering is the enemy, who is the father of lies, and who comes to kill and steal and destroy. God hates such things.

So why was God drawing my attention to these verses at this time? Wasn't it a bit harsh? Well, God treats us all as individuals, knowing each of us so well. It might not be appropriate for all, and I certainly wouldn't offer these verses as comfort to someone in a similar situation! However I can say that in a crazy sort of way I appreciated it and drew comfort from these verses. For a start, it ACKNOWLEDGED my pain. Emotional pain is invisible and most people just don't see it. I felt like I had just been in a road crash and broken every bone in my body, but instead of rushing me off to intensive care people seemed to think that if they left me alone for a bit I'd be up and running around again in a week or two. You simply can't see emotional damage, so people often don't recognise that it is there. God did. That in itself was helpful.

In all these references to suffering, too, there was hope. There was the hope that somehow, in some way, some good could come out of it. Impossible thought! What good could possibly come out of such gross pain, such awful devastation? Yet we know that God can work his strange alchemy in all situations. (Romans 8:28, NIV: "And we know that in all things God works for the good of those who love him.") It's at the heart of our faith. It's there for all to see in the cross. Out of extremes of pain and rejection came salvation, wholeness and healing for so many. The Man of Sorrows became the glorious Son of Man, to whom all authority in heaven and earth was given. The Victim became the Victor. He himself was amply rewarded, comforted, and restored to his former glories, with more added, if that is possible. God doesn't engineer the situation in order to produce these things, but, given that the suffering was already there as my new daily reality, it was a comfort to think that somehow there might possibly be some meaning in it. What had I got to lose? It seemed to me that I might as well get whatever good I could out of it! So I clung to these verses.

God doesn't promise to protect us from pain and suffering but he does promise never to leave us alone in it. "The Lord is close to those whose hearts are breaking" (Psalm 34:18, Living Bible). Sometimes we feel his presence, sometimes we don't. When we have lost someone we love – worse, when the one we love most in the world has left – this is not easy to believe. But God is faithful. He is also extremely patient. He knows what it is like to be abandoned. So he doesn't mind telling us again and again in as many different ways as he can that he will not abandon us. He told me that through people, through sermons, through Scripture, through words in a book like this, through music on the radio or heard in a shop. Time and time and time again he told me "I will not fail you or forsake you." It's written all over the Bible. One of the places is Deuteronomy 31:8, but it occurs in many others as well. In that first year I think I must have had every one of them drawn to my attention. I especially like the rendering of Hebrews 13:5 in the Amplified Version, because of its emphasis. It goes: "He [God] Himself has said, 'I will not in any way fail you nor give you up nor leave you without support. [I will] not, [I will] not, [I will] not in any degree leave you helpless nor forsake nor let you down (relax My hold on you)! [Assuredly not!]'"

In the darkness of one night these words went through my head and so I wrote them down:

> *When all else is gone,*
> *I am here.*
> *Faithful and strong,*
> *I am here.*
> *In the deep darkness of night,*
> *I'm with you,*
> *though just out of sight.*
> *Safe in the eye of the storm,*
> *My love keeps you safe, keeps you warm.*
> *My strength drives away every fear.*
> *Your God, your Refuge, is here.*

We ourselves cannot choose what happens to us; we cannot always avoid suffering, but we *can* choose how we respond to it. Suddenly I could identify with the prophet

Habakkuk (Chapter 3:16–19, Amplified Bible): "I will wait quietly for the day of trouble and distress. Though the fig tree does not blossom, and there is no fruit on the vines, though the product of the olive fails and the fields yield no food, though the flock is cut off from the fold and there are no cattle in the stalls, yet I will rejoice in the Lord; I will exult in the victorious God of my salvation!"

More often I could say with the psalmist, "O God, listen to me! Hear my prayer! For wherever I am, though far away at the ends of the earth, I will cry to you for help. When my heart is faint and overwhelmed, lead me to the mighty, towering rock of safety" (Psalm 61, Living Bible). Actually the truth is that most often I *couldn't* say that with the psalmist; it was far too long a prayer for me to muster! Often prayer was beyond me; I couldn't even frame the thoughts. At those times I prayed a sort of précis of those verses. This became my exclusive prayer for months and months. It was the only one that worked in this new, strange and confusing reality. In the middle of the nightmare it was a prayer that God NEVER once failed to answer. It was so useful I offer it to you. It went simply like this:

"Help!"

God *is* reality. If you've never known this, now's the time to try it out. Some might say you just need a crutch to lean on. Well, most people with broken legs do. And most people with broken hearts need a spiritual crutch. Look around, they've all got one. Some turn to drink, some turn to sex, some turn to working all hours of the day. Turning to God is simply less risky to your health and more effective than any of the above. Lean on him. He's big, he can take the strain, and he loves to help. I don't know why; it's just the way he is.

I had to cling to him; he was the only Reality I had.

Chapter 2

Will I Survive?

Will I survive the storm?

After the initial shock, the next reaction I felt was total emotional disintegration. I had never felt anything like it in my life before. My interior landscape shattered, blown into a thousand pieces. I could never understand how, in that state, I could still be walking around.

I felt so fragile. Like a shattered vase in that moment before it collapses, still holding its shape but crazed with cracks. So fragile. Don't touch me! Don't touch! I'll fall apart!

And then I do. Waves of emotion engulf me. Unbearable. Inexpressible. Grief that has you howling like a wounded animal. Despair that opens gulfs in your soul you never knew existed. Black chasms of emptiness beyond tears. Panic that has you running down the road. Literally. Running and running with no relief. This isn't an enemy you can run from.

Anger explodes ferociously when you least expect it. Murderous anger that clamours for expression, but has none. Minor sights, sounds and comments bring floods of tears and engulfing sadness. You can have six different overwhelming emotions a day. Or an hour. The storm plays loudly, howling in your ears, blowing you from one extreme to another. Life looks unreal. People look unreal. Why are they carrying on so normally? Are they really so blind to this raging storm? Yes, because it's raging in your heart. Unseen and inescapable. Totally out of control.

I had no warning that my husband was going to leave. However, about a month before he left I was accompanying a group of schoolchildren on a trip, and coming back in the coach we travelled through a violent storm. Looking back, that storm became a metaphor for me for the emotional storm I was about to pass through.

The storm

I was sitting in the front seat of the coach, surveying the miles of motorway in front of me and wondering how long it would be before we were home. It had been a long day and I was looking forward to the meal I knew my husband would have ready. The coachload of kids that I'd taken out for the day were being somewhat pacified by the video that was on for their entertainment, but stuck in the very front seat I couldn't see it, and I was bored.

So I started praying. Hadn't I been complaining that I hadn't enough time to pray? I was worried by my husband: he'd been acting strangely recently, and obviously there was something going on in his head that he hadn't got round to telling me about yet. I started to pray for him, thankful that prayer can be a silent, in-your-head activity. I closed my eyes and in my mind I talked to the God who knows all our thoughts, telling him my concerns and knowing that he, at least, understood the situation. When I opened my eyes the motorway vista still stretched out in front of me, but over to the right, from the fields to the sky, was the most amazing black storm cloud. It was like something a child would draw, a black ball of swirling cotton wool with streaks of lightning flashing through it. "Thank goodness we've missed that!" I thought. It looked dark and very angry. Then the road began to bend gently round to the right, and slowly but inexorably I realised that the road I was on was taking me directly towards the storm. We were going to have to travel through it.

It started with a gloriously sunny day turning into grey rain (not unusual for England, even in the summer), but the rain became more and more intense, falling in heavy lines that the windscreen wipers could barely deal with. Then the greyness turned the sunny afternoon into night and visibility became almost nil. I could hardly make out the car travelling a few yards in front of us. The coach was still hurtling on at what seemed to me to be a suicidal speed, but there was nothing I could do about it. The feeling of helplessness was intense. I glanced at the driver, who *seemed* to know what he was doing. The rest of the party were too engrossed in the video to worry about what the weather was doing outside. Then the lightning started. Huge forks flashed down to earth to the right and left, illuminating the crowded motorway with its cars battling through the driving rain. I started to get really frightened. Would we get hit by lightning? What would happen if one of those cars skidded on the wet road and caused a pile up? Wouldn't it be safer to get off the motorway and let such a storm pass? Couldn't the driver ease up just a little on that accelerator? I looked at him again, with more concern this time. I *hoped* he knew what he was doing. It was the worst storm I had ever experienced, and we were hurtling on through it as if it were not there! Disaster seemed inevitable.

The crash never came. Eventually we travelled through the worst of the storm, past the sheet lightning and immediate threat of danger into more grey rain. The colour had gone from the world; all was shadow. The darker slate-greys of trees were passing as if in formal procession and everything was monochrome, fields of greyness, details imperceptible, lost in the mist. Had we really started the journey in sunshine? The rain was still pouring out of the grey sky and bouncing off the grey road. The headlights of the coach made dirty yellow paths in the grey air and landed palely on the grey forms of the vehicles in front of us. Travelling at the same speed, they seemed immobile, grey shapes geometric in the grey rain. It seemed as if the weather had changed permanently and I settled down to endure rain and greyness for the rest of the long journey home.

Then, slowly, the rain started to ease off. The fields began to gain a tinge of green in their greyness. The windscreen wipers were less frenetic, passing in graceful, rhythmic arcs across the screen again. The miles passed, the rain lessened and suddenly there was a weak ray of sunlight. Slowly but surely we travelled through the storm and emerged once more into a glorious day of sunshine, with light all around and colour restored to the world.

In the next weeks, and months, and years, I clung to the memory of this experience. It reassured me that I *would* travel through this stage in my life.

A real-life metaphor

Of course my husband wasn't telling me what was going on in his mind. His mind was full of plans to leave me. In the days to come the storm I'd driven through became a metaphor for me for the emotional journey I was making.

When I saw the storm coming I thought it was going to miss me. I knew "marriage breakdown" and divorce were endemic in our society, but, like everyone else, I never thought it would happen to *me*! I think that made the storm, when it came, more difficult. People might think that in a divorce things are so bad that you can see the separation coming from a long way off. Maybe for some this is true, but for me there were no great warning signs, no big rows, just a quiet sense of unease and a strange loss of communication. Everything continued as normal. Sunny days of a happy marriage as they had been for 22 years. I was secure in such a history. I trusted in my husband's complete faithfulness. I trusted in my ability to raise issues and be honest with my husband. I trusted in God to be able to sort out any problems we might have. He always had done before.

But God allows people their own free will. He will not force anyone to change a decision they have made. We call God all-powerful, but he has chosen to limit his power by giving us autonomy over our own lives. When my husband decided to choose to go his own way, there was nothing I could do about it. He made that very clear to me.

There was nothing God could do about it, either. Except hold me.

When the storm rages, there is a sense of fear, a lack of control, as the lightning strikes all around you. A fatal accident seems inevitable. At this stage in the emotional storm I felt an acute fear of the future, and an overwhelming sense of being out of control.

It is like being tossed about in a stormy sea. It is wet and cold and frightening, and the noise and bluster drown out all else. Even God. Self-image is reduced to drowned-rat level. Your ears can't hear. Your eyes can't see. The storm buffets you about, strips you of your dignity. As everything you've ever clung to is ripped out of your hands and flies past your ears, you feel very vulnerable. There was a stage when that was how things were emotionally. So, after the first days of shock, numbness and denial there came for me a storm of emotions.

The trouble with the early days and weeks is that you can have all the symptoms of grief – loss, numb shock, overwhelming fear, raging anger, consuming guilt, dreadful sorrow, storms of tears – all in the same day or even the same *hour*. I never knew what was going to trigger another emotion, or which one it would be this time. It could be anything. Official letters from legal people, or an impending meeting with my spouse, were impossible hurdles, of course. But it could just as easily have been something very small, such as someone saying, "Look after yourself" (who else is going to look after me?), or the music on an advert. Some evocative scent or sight will do it. Families out for the day together. The other side of the bed still smooth and unslept-in. These things are unpredictable: you just don't know when they are going to hit you. Crying in the privacy of your own room is one thing, but crying in the middle of the supermarket takes some dealing with.

The overwhelming feeling is of lack of control. That is why work is such a relief, I think, if you are lucky enough to have it. The working environment for me was one where things were still as they had always been. Sometimes, getting lost in the minutiae of a sixth-form lesson, or dealing with a discipline problem, I forgot, for a whole ten minutes or half an hour even, the storm that was raging in my head. But when there was no work to occupy me the tears would come unbidden, overflowing and difficult to control. Yet they had to be controlled, because you can't cry at work. You can't cry at home, either, because the children get upset. Angry responses burst out, too. Like lightning they strike unpredictably and without warning. At this stage some people stopped speaking to me, quite rightly, since they never knew what sort of sharp response they'd get – an innocuous question such as "Doing anything special this weekend?" could result in sudden flashes of rage.

The storm distorts reality. I lived through a long time when life seemed very grey. I remember having the sinking feeling that the whole journey of life was now going to be like this, with little enjoyment and even less hope. (I have written about this in more detail in chapter five.) I think that this is actually the most dangerous part of the storm. Outbursts of emotion look dramatic and painful, because they are, but in a crazy way they are proof that you are still alive and kicking. When hope dies there seems little point in being alive.

Finally, there is the dawning realisation that the rain is at last easing off. Imperceptibly at first, and much more slowly than I ever would have imagined, I emerged into the sunshine, which is really the focus of this book. There is joy in my life now, real confident happiness that other people notice, and that I would never have believed possible. There is joy such as I've never known before, and a security in God. The last five years have been like travelling through that storm. I emerged into full sunshine again, and after a few miles the road dried off and it was as if the storm had never been. Yes, it is a surprisingly long process and people travel through the storm at different rates. But the storm will not last for ever. It does get better. Often, progress is only obvious in retrospect. There is a progression, but at the time it doesn't always seem like that. A minor incident or comment can throw you, and it seems that you have come nowhere. It is weeks, months or years since your partner went and still you haven't adjusted to it! However, the violence of the emotions becomes less intense and the gaps between bouts greater. As you look back you can see clearly how far you have come.

But at first I was devastated.

The devastation

Devastated. It is the right word. Everything you have known is in ruins. Devastated. Destroyed. Barren. Your home, your family, your social life, your sex life, your emotions, your self-esteem, your prayer life. All devastated. Your trust in that one special person, your trust in all people, your trust in God. Devastated. If the one who knows you so well, better than anyone, can't love you, who can? Can God even? But you can't even bear to look at that one yet. If God has so much as a flicker of doubt about you you'll not only be devastated, you'll be utterly destroyed.

In the devastation you are powerless. Powerless to change a thing. Powerless to win him back. Powerless to make him love you. No glue mends a broken family. You are powerless to soothe the hurt and confusion in your children's eyes. Powerless to stop the determined approach of the law that will sever you permanently. Powerless to prevent the loss. You don't even have power over yourself. Emotions hit you unbidden and overcome you against your will. You pray and pray but the agony continues. There is no last-minute rescue here. You fight and fight but the onslaught is too great. You might as well brace yourself to hold back an advancing tank. Superman might be able to do it, but you are not Superman. Or Super*woman*. You haven't got the strength. You have two options: get out of the way or get crushed. So you get out of the way and watch the tank rumble on, crushing all that is precious to you. Leaving devastation.

Where is the hope in all this?

To begin with, there is none. The only glimmer of hope you begin to discern in the darkness is God. The rebuilder of ancient ruins. The Restorer. God really is in the business of restoration.

God is in control

God is in control – he sent me the real storm as a warning and a sign of the emotional storm that was coming. He knew in advance what was going to happen, even if I didn't. I found that thought comforting.

When I was in the middle of the emotional storm Isaiah 54 kept coming to me. You know the sort of thing:

the preacher's text at church on Sunday is Isaiah 54, and then it turns up in your daily readings. A friend phones and says, "Have you read Isaiah 54?" and then the cat knocks over your Bible and it falls open at page 752 – yes, you've guessed it – Isaiah 54.

I finally decided I'd better take a good look at it. Isaiah 54 was written about 550 BC and it shows that human nature hasn't changed a lot since then. The writer of the passage refers in verse six to a wife who married young, only to be rejected in later life. It's a metaphor here, but at least it shows that the idea was understood even then. It made me realise that God has seen it all before. The husbands who in mid-life fall for the younger woman, the women who cheat on their husbands, the violence and abuse that masquerade as love. He's seen it all before. Millions of times. Even if he didn't know each of us individually and intimately, he would know the process through observation over the aeons. He understands the process, and is skilled in dealing with it. To you or me it is completely new and frightening. We don't know which way to turn. To God it is very familiar, and he knows exactly how to handle it. God is expert at sorting out the messes people constantly make.

God has immense power. He limits his power in order to give us free will. Without free will there can be no true love. But, nevertheless, he has enormous power, and if we surrender our lives to him he will take over. He won't override our free will but he can and will control our lives if we let him. This whole situation was too big for me but it was not beyond God.

My experience is that if you give yourself and your life to God he will tenderly and expertly restore. There is one thing you can say about this period. The emotions come unexpectedly and uncontrollably but they do pass. You soon learn that one emotion can just as quickly be replaced with another. That's the exhausting part.

However, the point is that they come but they go again. So it is with this whole stage. It will pass. Emotional stability will come again. On 25th October 1998 he gave me this passage from Job 11:16–19 (Amplified Bible): "For you shall forget your misery; you shall remember it as waters that pass away. And your life shall be clearer than the noonday... you shall lie down and none shall make you afraid."

I didn't believe it then. I do now. I didn't believe it then because it didn't *feel* as if the storm would ever pass. But feelings do pass. The facts are that if you have given your life to God he is irrevocably committed to you, whether you believe it or not, whether you feel it or not. It's not to do with you or your behaviour, it's to do with him. As he says in Isaiah 54:10 (NIV), "Though the mountains be shaken and the hills be removed, yet my unfailing love for you will not be shaken nor my covenant of peace be removed."

What's more, God is immensely powerful, "The Lord Almighty", "The God of the whole Earth". Infinite power mixed with infinite tenderness and compassion. What a combination! You are safe in his hands. He is all-powerful and all-loving. Always. There is nowhere safer.

Isaiah 54 is about restoration. Without minimising the pain, it offers hope of a new life. When all seems in chaos around you, the hope of a new life can be a real anchor in the storm. Verse eleven sums up the whole chapter for me: "O you afflicted! Storm-tossed and not comforted. I will build you with stones of turquoise and lay your foundations with sapphires" (Amplified Bible). God sees things as they are. He doesn't try to make out that they are better than they seem, or that you should be feeling better than you are. "Afflicted, storm-tossed and not comforted" – yes, that was me all right, as a diary entry of the time shows:

What an awful, awful week. I felt so alone! I got stressed out and twisted up with hurt and insecurity and exhaustion and panic and fear. I hate living like this!... Everything is so second-rate. Even chocolate! Especially alcohol! Nothing satisfies! Friends' words clang tinnily. Their advice jars on my pain. Television is shown up for the cheap deception it is, saccharine-sweet instead of nourishing. A clanging cardboard cut-out representing reality. Sleep is evasive. A warm bath fills time but brings no peace. I don't like the waves of confusion. I hate the constant struggling to find reality. Only God satisfies. Only God brings sanity and peace in this storm.

When things are this bad, the normal comforts don't work any more. But as well as acknowledging the reality of my situation, Isaiah 54 goes on to offer hope of restoration in the middle of the devastation. "I will (re) build you with stones of turquoise, your foundations with sapphires." I happen to love the colour blue. Can you imagine it! If the foundations in this building, which are never even seen, are to be of sapphires, what will the walls be like? The next verse tells us: "I will make your battlements of rubies, your gates of sparkling jewels, and all your walls of precious stones." Here is God's plan for rebuilding/restoration/repair of storm damage. This is "above and beyond" stuff, isn't it? It's an extravagant metaphor from an extravagant God.

What are you looking for to restore your house? Wood? Granite? Flint? Sandstone? Common brick? Forget it! God is building in jewels! The end of Revelation, chapter 21, makes it even clearer. This *is* God's building style. Layer on layer of precious stones. Gates carved out of huge pearls. Walls overlaid with gold. Extravagance!

There are splendid buildings in this world: the Taj Mahal, the Dome of the Rock in Jerusalem, the splendour of the baroque cathedrals, every inch gilded and painted.

These are breathtaking, but how can even the greatest artist or architect compare with the creative genius of God? Who can imagine what this building will be like? I've never seen anything similar. Who knows what God is preparing for me, for us? Whatever it is, it will be good. That's British understatement. It'll be amazingly, breathtakingly, joyfully bejewelled. It'll be God's building. Riches beyond imagining. Sometimes I fear the future. There's no need to fear *this* future. This generosity is overwhelming. When God restores or rebuilds, he does it in style.

He can and will restore the devastated places in your life, if you will allow him to. The tears and the turmoil are a season in your life. Take it from me: the rest of your life will not be like this.

Let's finish with a classic, so often quoted it is practically a cliché, but none the less true for that. Jeremiah 29:11 (NIV) reads: "For I know the plans I have for you," declares the LORD, "plans to prosper you and not to harm you, plans to give you hope and a future." Yes!

Chapter 3

Was It My Fault?

As you look at the endless damage, there is one big question:

Why?

Or rather why? why? why? why? why? why? why? why? why? why? why? why?

This year my parents celebrated their Golden Wedding anniversary. Some teenagers today do not believe it is possible to stay faithful to one person for fifty years, for a lifetime. As far as I was concerned that was not only possible, it was the norm. As a teenager I had a strong religious faith. So did the man I wanted to marry. We took our vows in front of God very sincerely, and expected to keep them for life. As our parents had. All relationships have ups and downs, but we weathered them. Then my husband left me. There had been no abuse, no history of affairs on either side, no huge financial problems, no addictions, no crimes or prison sentences, no serious problems at all, I thought. I looked at our life: we had what most people were longing for. One friend had laughingly commented that we were the only functioning family she knew. Then he left, and the family ceased to function in the way it had for so long. It seems he had only one problem. Me.

So starts the endless cycle of "why?". It goes on day and night. Your mind demands a reason. If that wasn't love, what *is*? If you can't believe him, whom can you believe? If your trust in the one you know best has failed, how can you ever trust again? You sift everything that has ever happened from the day you met to the day he went, looking for clues. Looking for a solution. Looking for reasons.

I'm not going to tell you the debate I went through in my mind. I know all my weaknesses, all my faults and all my negative character traits, but I don't see why you should as well. It is enough to say that when my marriage failed they all came home to me in sharp relief and Glorious Technicolor, and in their wake they left a chasm of guilt. "All have fallen and come short of the glory of God" (Romans 3:23). I wasn't going to argue with that. Deep down, we all know this is true. If you'd ever thought you had any character deficiencies, this is the time when they come glaringly to your attention. Everything critical that anyone ever said to you appears to have been proven true.

The key word here is failure. It is one of the euphemisms for divorce, isn't it? "When my marriage failed." It sounds less harsh than "when we divorced" or "when he left me". Yet failure implies fault, and fault brings guilt, and guilt leads to shame.

When my marriage failed I felt that I had let everyone down. *I had let myself down.* Whether I sued for divorce or agreed to his divorce plans, I was going against my own principles and values. *I had let my husband down*, for obviously I had failed to be a good enough wife to him. *I had let my children down* by being unable to sort out my problems with their father, knowing the pain that would be theirs. *I had let society down:* I was now one of those awful statistics that one in three marriages fail. *I had let God down,* because I had promised before God to stay faithfully married to this one man for life.

What a weight of guilt! What a weight of shame! It is heavy enough to crush some completely, and it clings to us all like a heavy grey cloak, an extra weight to carry around on top of all the grief. What I didn't realise for a long, long time is that there are two types of guilt, justified and unjustified: the guilt we are responsible for and the guilt we are *not* responsible for. Nor did I understand that there are ways of dealing with both.

Justified and unjustified guilt

We don't like acknowledging our guilt because it brings with it a fear of punishment. So first I have to tell you the good news. Jesus has already taken our punishment. There is no punishment left for Christians. 1 John 1:9 (NIV) says, "If we confess our sins, he [God] is faithful and just and will forgive us our sins and purify us from all unrighteousness." God is faithful because he sticks to the agreement that he made with Jesus, that he would take his offering of himself as a sacrifice so great that it would take away the sins of the people. "He was pierced for our transgressions, he was crushed for our iniquities" (Isaiah 53:5, NIV). It's already done. God cannot give you the punishment when he has already given it to someone else: it wouldn't be fair. Whatever pain you are suffering now, it is not punishment laid on you for things you have done wrong.

Why would Jesus willingly take the punishment? Because he knew that by giving himself in exchange for our sin he could eternally gain a love relationship with millions of people, bringing them back to the Father. He did it because he knew he would gain *us*, that's you and me, for as it says in Isaiah 53:10 (NIV): "though the LORD makes his life a guilt offering, he will see his offspring and prolong his days". Then there's 1 Peter 2:24 (NIV): "He himself bore our sins in his body on the tree, so that we might die to sins and live for righteousness." This is an amazing thought for all those who have been abused by men. Here is a man, a real man who, rather than inflict abuse on you, loves you enough to take it himself. As he himself said on the night before he died, "This is my *body* given for you." Just a thought.

"God made him who had no sin to be sin for us, so that in him we might become the righteousness of God," proclaims Paul in 2 Corinthians 5:21 (NIV). Becoming a Christian is to make yourself part of this agreement. For those of you readers who are Christians, this is your inheritance. This is the free gift given to you. Take it. There is nothing to do or say, except "thank you". If you are *not* in on this agreement with God I have one piece of advice for you – check it out! It's available to all and it's a very good deal. So, "therefore, there is now no condemnation for those who are in Christ Jesus" (Romans 8:1, NIV). When God convicts he doesn't condemn. The Holy Spirit's job is to make people aware of where they are going wrong so that the loving relationship between them and God can be restored.

Realistic guilt is a healthy thing. Yes, really! Guilt is a warning signal that tells us when we have done something wrong. We can then do something about it, seek forgiveness from God, accept the forgiveness God gives us, forgive ourselves and move on without being burdened by it. Forgiveness is amazingly precious. It frees us; it wipes the slate clean; it gives us the opportunity to start again; it restores relationship, and it takes the weight off our shoulders. It's a very beautiful thing. God forgives me; he doesn't have to but he does, freely and generously. I treasure that.

Unrealistic guilt is an unhealthy thing. As well as carrying justified guilt for the things we *are* responsible for, we also carry a load of unjustified guilt. That is, guilt for things we are not responsible for. Guilt when carried for too long leads to shame. It took me four and a half years to be able to say, "I am *divorced*." Why? Because I was ashamed of it. As I argue in chapter nine, if you divorce your husband or wife for a trivial reason, that is a shameful thing. However, Scripture itself shows that it is not wrong to divorce for a valid reason. My conscience is clear. I did everything I could to preserve my marriage. I put off the legal divorce and left the door open for reconciliation for as long as possible. For three years I waited and prayed. But in the end it takes two to make a relationship, and if the other person will not co-operate with you there is nothing more that you can do. I have finally come to see that I do not need to carry the shame that is put on me by society. The big, unspecified "they" may think it's a shameful thing to be divorced, but that is their problem. The church itself may think it is a shameful thing to be divorced, but I respectfully request them to study all that Scripture has to say on the subject thoroughly (see chapter nine for more on this). Some people in the church used to think it was a shameful thing to be black. It is not. I have in the past thought of myself as a lesser being because I am female. I am not any the less in God's eyes for being female or black, British, Ugandan, Japanese or Inuit, married, single or divorced.

In the end, it is what God thinks about us that counts. From time to time people will judge you because of their own prejudices or ignorance. You do not have to accept their judgement. I think of it as unsolicited mail. A large parcel arrives on your doorstep. The carrier says, "Sign here". The parcel has your name on it; it has been delivered to your door but you have not ordered it. You do not have to sign for it. If you have not ordered the goods, if you do not want them, if you do not want to pay for them, you do not have to accept them. Return to sender. Why have unwanted parcels cluttering up your hallway? If anyone tries to deliver unjustified guilt to your door, don't accept it.

There is another type of unjustified guilt we carry: the guilt that results from the accusations thrown at us by our partners. After all, they are the ones who know us best, aren't they? If any of these are justified accusations, don't panic – there is a way out. You simply say sorry to those you have harmed, ask for their forgiveness and change your behaviour. You may not get forgiveness from people, but that's their problem; you've taken responsibility for what is yours. You will always get forgiveness from God. But, before you go around asking forgiveness from everyone, have a think. Is this really your fault? What most of us eventually realise is that a lot of what is thrown at us is unjustified. This is because of an interesting phenomenon that psychologists call "projection". I experienced this before I knew the word for it. I used to feel as if I were going around with a full-length mirror in front of me. Shortly before my husband left, when I had no idea anything was wrong, I experienced a moment like this: I was once looking lovingly at him, thinking how good he was looking in those new clothes he'd just bought, when he caught my gaze. Instead of returning the loving look as I expected, his expression turned to disgust and he said, "Why are you looking at me as if I am dirt?" I was amazed! Nothing had been further from my mind, but it did no good to explain that. It was crazy! It happened so often that I began to feel I had an invisible mirror in front of me. "I love you!" I'd say. "No you don't, you hate me," he'd reply. It felt as if he were looking at me but seeing himself. It is very confusing to be on the end of projected feelings; you really don't know if the accusation is true or not. One incident suddenly made it very clear to me. It was late one night, after the kids had gone to bed, about a fortnight before he actually left. I was very emotional. I suppose I was pleading for our marriage. I was really pleading for our relationship. I let him see how much losing him was hurting me. I reminded him of all the love we'd shared: was it really worth throwing all that away? He did not see it that way. He did not see me as his best friend, his lover. He began to tell me exactly how he *did* see me. In the end he said, "... and you are so SUPERFICIAL." He was being completely serious. At that point my emotions did an about-turn and a back-flip and I went from distraught tears to laughter in a moment. It was genuine laughter. He was very surprised. He didn't see what was so funny. Superficial? You can call me many things, but superficial is not one of them! No one who has known me for more than ten minutes would call me superficial. I KNEW I wasn't a superficial person. At that moment I began to see that not everything he said about me was true.

One way of coping with your own guilt is to project it on to someone else. If you are not prepared to take responsibility for your own decisions, you blame someone else. I meet many men and women travelling through life still weighed down by the thought that if they had been a stone lighter or a stone heavier, done more washing up, less yoga, had more sex, had less sex, not spent so much money, spent more time with the kids, prayed harder, jogged more, etc. etc., s/he wouldn't have left them. What I would like to say to them is this: Honestly, it's probably unrealistic guilt. Return to sender. Or at least just bin it. Drop it. Leave it. It's not yours. You don't have to carry it.

Forgiveness

The whole of Romans chapter three is about how no one, Jew or Gentile, has fully kept the law. Psalm 14:3 says, "No one is righteous, no not one." This is the truth. This is the bottom line. No one is righteous. We don't see it this way. We tend to see it as a righteousness graph. I am not fully good but I'm 98% there, or 55% there, or (on a bad day) 25% there, but I'm still better than Hitler. Hitler was only 2% there. The problem is that if the pass mark is perfection then in this exam even 99.9% won't pass. We all know that we are not perfect. So in effect we are all in the same boat. The Queen of England, the president, a drug dealer, an animal lover, a good person, a thief, the nicest person you know, all have fallen short of the glory of God. None of us are up to standard. None of us have hit the mark. So none of us have the right to judge another. When they brought the woman caught in adultery to Jesus, he said that the one who had not sinned should throw the first stone. To hold unforgiveness against someone is to hold judgement against them. In Matthew 7 (NIV), Jesus says, "Do not judge, or you too will be judged. For in the same way as you judge others, you will be judged, and with the measure you use, it will be measured to you." Excuse me a moment. "AAARRRRGGGGHHHH!"

That's better. This teaching is hard to take on board. Not intellectually, I can deal with it intellectually, but emotionally. How can God demand such an attitude from us? Does he know how much it hurts? Doesn't he see how unfair it is? Can't he see that some people act worse than others? Is he going to just stand there and let them get away with it? The answers to those questions are yes, yes, yes, NO! To forgive someone is not to let them off the hook. It is to put them on God's hook. In releasing the one you are forgiving, you are letting go of them and putting them into God's hands. He is the only one without sin. He is the judge of all mankind. He will deal with it. Release it *to* him.

Forgiveness is not being walked over

Maybe here it is worth saying a few things about what forgiveness is NOT. Forgiving someone doesn't mean you have to carry on being a victim of their bad behaviour. Forgiveness doesn't mean you lie down and get walked on. That is not a loving thing to do; it shows a lack of respect for yourself and it deceives them into thinking they can continue the behaviour without consequences. Then they simply end up hurting more people in the same way, and eventually hurt themselves. We must be willing to forgive, but that doesn't mean we have to carry on tolerating dysfunctional behaviour. Forgiveness does not mean we have to passively accept disloyalty from trusted friends, betrayal from our spouse, abuse from family members or malpractice from professional workers. You may forgive your family and friends for bad-mouthing you, but you don't have to carry on listening to it. You may forgive your spouse for the pain of betrayal, but you don't have to entertain their lover in your house, or carry on living as husband and wife if they refuse to give up the other person. You may forgive the family member who hit you, or worse, but you do not have to stick around to put up with more of the same. You may forgive professional workers whose thoughtlessness or poor practice causes you pain, but you don't have to put up with malpractice or injustice if there is something that can be done about it. In short, to forgive doesn't mean you exempt people from taking responsibility for their own actions.

Act like royalty

I wish I could draw. When people hurt you, all sorts of reactions and retaliations rise up in you. I didn't know how to react to what my husband had done, so God gave me a picture in my mind to help me. This is where I wish I could draw. Have you ever seen a young dad lying on the rug watching television with his little kid? Or maybe outside on a summer's day, lying on the grass watching a ball game? The picture was like that. Dad was lying on his left elbow, head resting on his hand. The kid was really little, just a toddler, sat in the space made between Dad's chest and curled-round knees, surrounded, protected.

Dad's right arm was around her. The picture was very relaxed, yet the expression on Dad's face as they watched is difficult to describe: it was serious, with a wash of sadness somehow. Totally relaxed and in control, and yet not happy with what he was seeing and quietly protective of his little girl. The little girl was getting upset because some other kids in the park had started taunting her and calling her names. She began to get agitated and started sticking her tongue out and thumbing her nose back at them. Dad gently squeezed her shoulder, drawing her in to him, and she looked at him. Her attention drawn away from the other kids, she realised that Daddy was there, and that he saw them too, and that he wasn't pleased. Then he simply said to her, "Act like royalty."

Act like royalty. Royalty are extremely privileged but they have a lot to put up with too! People taunt and jeer and take the mickey. The press search for weaknesses that they can exploit, invading their privacy and provoking them to get a reaction that will make a good photograph to publish. From an early age the young princes and princesses are taught to act like royalty, to ignore the taunts and not to retaliate. To imitate the behaviour of the older members of the royal family. Surrounded by every privilege, protected by bodyguards, with all the resources of money and power at their fingertips, it would be demeaning for them to react like an ordinary kid from the street. You get the picture?

We are members of the ultimate royal family. The King of Kings is our Dad. He is secure in his authority. All the resources of his kingdom are available to us, his much-loved children. God was saying to me: act like royalty.

Forgiveness is an ongoing process

God is only asking us to do what he himself does. He plays by his own rules. He simply wants us to imitate him, our own Father. If we have been forgiven much, then we should forgive other people.

This doesn't mean pretend you haven't been hurt. It's worse than that – it means look at exactly how badly you have been hurt and *then* forgive. The ultimate example of forgiveness came from the lips of Jesus, in the middle of his mental and physical torture, when speech itself was almost an impossibility. "Father, forgive them, they don't know what they are doing!" To accept the fact that you are hurting and then let go of your resentment about it and your wish to retaliate in kind is real forgiveness.

The trouble, I found, is that the hurt is ongoing. So the forgiveness has to be ongoing. It's not just when you realise that you are now alone, for example, that you have to forgive, but on all the subsequent occasions when loneliness kicks in. Christmas spent alone, your birthday, holiday times, going to an empty bed, seeing couples out together, and the party at work that you haven't got a partner to take to. Each time it hurts again in a different way, and each time you have to let it go. It's an ongoing and often repeated process, but it does get easier.

Now, let's get to the real reason for forgiveness, the really *selfish* one: It helps YOU. We've all met men and women embittered by their experiences, sour-faced and hard-hearted. I really didn't want to be like that. It's only as we let go of the hurt and leave it behind, leave it to God, that we can move on. We can't rebuild a new life if we are still tied by unforgiveness to the old. How God helped me on that one I explain in chapter six.

In the end I found I had to leave the question "Why?" behind. It wasn't a very useful question. A more productive question was, "Where do I go from here?"

Chapter 4

What Do I Tell Other People?

The ongoing pain

In a way, the storm of emotions and the endless questioning were easier to bear than the next stage. At least the emotions broke out dramatically, and people realised something was wrong and were kind. At least the questioning kept my mind active and I felt alive.

But after a time the pain crystallised into the realisation of what had actually happened. The panic is over; the stunned disbelief has passed; you've looked for reasons and answers and found none, and now this pain is here to stay. I felt as if I had been mortally wounded. It was as if a sword had passed through me. Right through the core of my being. Not just into my heart, but right out the other side. I couldn't even lie down. There was no rest from it. And it hurt. Sharply. Deeply. Constantly. And I lived with it.

Sometimes people noticed. "You've got a sword sticking all the way through you!" they'd say.

"Yes, I know."

"How do you manage to walk around like that?"

"I don't know."

When they see the wound, reactions vary. Many, horrified, move on quickly. Some stare, macabrely fascinated, appalled. The kindest look into your eyes, and you see in *their* eyes the tears that match your own. There is comfort there. At least these know there is nothing they can do. Some don't yet know that.

"You've got a sword going through you! Why don't you pull it out? Here, let me!" And they grab the handle and twist.

I don't know how I survived those moments. I quickly learnt to protect myself, sometimes graciously, sometimes not. "Don't touch! Please don't touch!"

The question why

One way that people twisted the sword in me was by constantly asking me "Why?" The trouble was, *I* might have worked out that the question "Why?" was not productive, but my friends and family were still struggling with it.

Telling other people was like watching ripples in a pond. First the sheer shock. The disbelief. Then the emotional reaction and the questioning. This all just exacerbated the pain. In many ways it's easier not to tell people. Some of the people who understood best what I was going through, and were therefore safe to tell, were those who had been bereaved. There are many similarities between the loss of a partner through divorce and the loss of a partner through bereavement. The grieving process, the overwhelming loss, the readjustment to life without them, the storms of emotions – all are similar. However, a sudden and unexpected death is treated with sympathy. A sudden and unexpected divorce is not. I cannot imagine telling anyone that my husband had just died and their reacting with the words, "What did you do to lose him?", "Never mind, he'll soon be back", "Well, it must have been six of one and half a dozen of the other", or "Think of all the extra time you'll have now – I'd love to have some time to myself". All of which were said to me when my husband left of his own free will.

I've been to three funerals in the last five years, and I cried at all of them. I cried for the loss of a friend and I cried for the husband or wife left behind. I know only too well what it is like to lose the person you love most in the world. I must admit that I also cried out of anger and jealousy. I was angry with society in general because I too had suffered the loss of my husband but had been treated very differently. I was jealous of the bereaved spouse for two reasons: first because they were honoured whereas I had been shamed, and second because they had a chance to celebrate the good things about their now-ended marriage.

This shame question is a big one, because if you say you are divorced the first reaction in the mind of the hearer is always, "Whose *fault* was it?" I have been known to try and forestall the debate with a litany of possibilities: "No, I didn't refuse him sex; no, I wasn't a career woman; I didn't neglect the family; I didn't spend too much money, and I have never had a toyboy." It's not a technique I recommend, but it certainly brings the unspoken thoughts out into the open.

Emotional pain lasts more than three weeks

In one memorial service I was struck by the plea of the bereaved wife: "We need your prayers; we can feel them now, but when *a month* has passed, please remember to keep praying for us." She's so right. That's one of the things that divorced and bereaved people have in common. After a year most people have forgotten about it, but you have barely acknowledged the reality of it. You've had one Christmas season without them, one uncelebrated wedding anniversary, one holiday where you tried to have a holiday alone, his/her birthday came and went, celebrated with others. Your birthday came and you wondered how to celebrate it.

Then there is the first anniversary of the day they left: the weather is similar; the feelings come rushing back, but you've survived! You've done everything once. Just once.

Two years go by and you've done everything *twice*. The legal work may or may not be settled. You may be a long way through the process of grief or a very short way down that road. People take varying amounts of time to recover. But to the world *at large* it's all in the past now. People judge a pain by their own experience. Unless they themselves have suffered a great loss, they will have no idea of how long it takes to adjust.

I was talking some months ago to a lady at a school parents' evening. She told me some of the pain she and her daughters were going through, pain so intense that she couldn't withhold the tears even in such a public place, pain destructive enough to seriously and noticeably disrupt her daughter's progress at school, yet a pain that went daily unacknowledged and unrecognised. On the same day I had overheard a teacher complaining about this girl's lack of work. She prefaced her comments with, "I know her parents split up, but that was *years* ago!" Two years ago, in fact. People just don't understand. It's been two years and the nightmare *still* isn't over. We haven't all woken up yet. Dad hasn't come to his senses, got over his little infatuation and returned. It's been two years and now it seems that one daughter will always live with Mum and one with Dad. So she's lost a sister as well as a father. Two years of trying to explain to Dad that she doesn't like this new woman and this weekend the new woman is moving into a new house with her father, permanently. He has put his own daughter aside and chosen *her* instead! Two years and Mum and Dad are still arguing over the financial arrangements and the solicitors keep ringing up and Mum cries but tries to pretend she doesn't. Two whole years of Mum crying; will she ever get over it and, if not, who will look after her? Two years and she still hasn't got her Mum back, not the Mum she used to know.

Two years and now she's feeling so weak and tired that the doctor says she's got ME but it's six months since she had that glandular fever and the Internet says that people with ME never totally recover. It's been two years and she loves her Dad, but if he really moves in with *her* this weekend she's NEVER going to visit him again. Two years! Will it be better or worse when they actually get divorced? And what's the point of getting up and going to school today – the science teacher will only scream at her again because her notes are not up to date, but she can't use the excuse of "family problems" again, she's been using that excuse for years. Two years in fact.

No cut-off point

At least most people accept that death is final. The problem with separation and divorce is that there is no cut-off point. While your partner is still alive people find it very hard to accept that the marriage is dead. There is no funeral. There is no shared grieving for the loss. This leaves you having to endure the pain while seeing no end to it. How long does this go on for? How long do you hold the door open? How long do you stay in the excruciating position of hoping that the person you love will return to you?

In case you think I am making too much of this, let me recount for you an incident that happened to me nearly five years after my husband had left.

I had seen my ex-husband unexpectedly that week, and it had upset me. (I call that the alien-in-my-husband's-body experience. It looks like that familiar person you know and love so well, but it doesn't take much – a look or a word, a passing expression – to make you realise that there is now a different person in that familiar body.) I was a bit unnerved by that experience, so on Sunday, when I found myself in an unfamiliar church and prayer ministry was offered at the end of the service, I went up for prayer. I explained briefly to the kindly and experienced stranger in this unfamiliar church and she began to pray. Half way through the prayer I stopped her, because she had begun to pray that God would bring him back to me.

"Has God told you to pray that?" I asked incredulously, my emotions suddenly going into turmoil. It had taken me the best part of five years to adjust to the fact that he'd gone!

"No, I haven't had a specific word on it," she answered.

I said that he didn't want reconciliation, and she said that God could change him! I explained all about God's not contravening man's free will, but it seemed to make no difference. In order to explain the magnitude of what she was asking, I said that I really thought reconciliation was impossible. She said God can do the impossible.

All the pain of the previous five years hit me. I wasn't at all sure that I wanted God to do the impossible, but I didn't dare say that in case she started to talk to me about forgiveness! Well-meaning people just don't seem to hear what you are saying.

I searched for a way to explain it to her. In the end I said that GOD wasn't telling me to pray for him to come back; he was telling me to leave the past and walk into the future with him. Even then she seemed to think that that was some sort of psychological trick – oh yes, God DID want me to leave the past so that I could leave it entirely open for him to do what he wanted – which might be to bring him back. No wonder people leave the church! I even explained how much the conversation we were having was tearing me in two (I'd gone up for prayer because I was already feeling vulnerable!) and how that attitude trapped me in an impossible position – unable to move on. I thought I'd got through then. "Oh..." she said, understanding finally dawning. "You can't move on... so it's like a bereavement!"

"Yes, it's like a bereavement," I said, relieved that she understood at last, "and in some ways it's worse..."

"...because you can't leave the past behind," she finished for me.

"At last!" I thought. But it STILL didn't stop her praying that God should bring him back *if it was his will*, whilst telling me I had to leave the past!

I was well on the way to recovery – articulate, well versed in theology and quite secure in my position, yet I found the experience very disturbing. I was concerned for what might happen to those less secure than myself. So I contacted one of the elders of the church whom I knew personally and he put me in touch with the leader of the ministry team. What surprised me was that neither saw the problem. Surely there was no harm in praying for God to reconcile the marriage? Surely that was a good thing to pray? I had to go through the whole reasoning process again, but they still didn't get it. "Look!" I said in the end. "When revival comes to this country, people are going to start raising the dead. What are we going to say to our bereaved people then? Imagine a woman comes to you some time after her husband has died, upset because she's just seen a video of their old life together.

"'Let's pray that God raises him from the dead,' the minister will suggest.

"'But that's impossible!' she'll reply.

"'Nothing's impossible for God,' is the answer.

"'But WE'VE HAD THE FUNERAL,' she'll say.

"'Ah yes, but God can raise the dead!'

"'...but he's buried – the body will be rotting by now!'

"'Didn't Martha say, "But, Lord, there'll be a stench"? – Yet Jesus still raised Lazarus,' the minister will argue incontrovertibly...'"

By the time I got to this point in my illustration, both the elder and the ministry-team leader were laughing at the ludicrousness of the picture and the insensitivity of it.

But I wasn't laughing. I pointed out that the effect on me of praying for my husband to return was exactly the same. "If God has given you the faith to believe that he will heal my marriage, then go ahead and pray for me," I said, "but first think about the magnitude of what you are doing; it is on the scale of raising the dead."

I think they began to get it.

I've told you this true story to show just how difficult it can be sometimes to get any sort of closure.

Closure

It's this whole process of educating people at the same time as hurting that's so difficult. This lack of understanding manifests itself in a tendency to minimise the pain, to judge, and to leave the divorced with no opportunity for closure. I began to ask myself why people found it so difficult to accept the idea that my happy Christian marriage was over. I came to the conclusion that many felt threatened by the break-up of my marriage, thinking, "If it happened to them it could happen to anyone – it could happen to *us*!" Such a thought is too awful to bear, so they continue to believe that there will be a reconciliation, way beyond the time when such a thing is possible. Reconciliations *do* happen. Praise God! But there are cases where a reconciliation would be downright wrong. (See Frank Retief's excellent book *Divorce*, chapter five; and chapter nine of this book.) It is wrong to send a person back into a situation of violence or abuse. This is often well understood. What are not so well understood are the cases where reconciliation is impossible. These cases are not always the most dramatic. If your spouse simply refuses to discuss the matter of reconciliation, there is nothing anyone can do about it. As my mother used to say, "It takes two to tango." If your partner chooses not to dance, you can't dance a tango by yourself.

Many people have told me that God can do the impossible. I think it is meant to be comforting, but actually it is just turning the knife. Many people in the church do divorcées a disservice by trying to resurrect a marriage that has already died. There comes a point when other people must recognise the final end to the relationship, in order to allow life to begin again. This is especially true in the case of the partner who didn't want the divorce. As any bereaved person knows, it is incredibly hard to let the person you love go and readjust to life without them.

The buzzword for this is "closure". It is necessary to close the door on the past before you can walk into the future. It is necessary to leave one place before you can move to the next. It is very, very difficult to gain closure on a situation if well-meaning people are constantly holding out the possibility of the restoration of the marriage. Of course you must hold the door open for reconciliation and restoration, especially at the beginning. Who knows what God might do? There are wonderful accounts of miraculous reconciliations and healings of marriages. I think I have heard them all. But I wish I could explain to friends, family and church the incredible tension involved in loving someone who has rejected you. To remain open and welcoming to them, and watch them walk away at the same time, calls for immense courage and endurance. It is awful to see hatred or scorn in the eyes of your enemy. It is absolutely devastating to see it in the eyes of your best friend. The psychological strain is extreme. It feels as if you are being torn in two. The song asks, "What can I do to make you love me?" For many of us the awful answer is, "Nothing".

If you are reading this out of interest, or because of a desire to help someone, let me tell you that a divorced person doesn't need your judgement of the situation. Believe me, they've sifted the evidence over and over again. The jury in their mind has considered the evidence for hours and hours on end, for days, for years. There is not one angle you could come up with that they haven't already considered in detail. What do you think they do in all those long nights when sleep evades them? A divorced person doesn't need your judgement; he or she needs your acceptance, your support and your love. Above all, he or she needs desperately to know that they are an OK person. They will have been told in considerable detail, by the person that knows them best, that they most definitely are not.

Boundaries

But if you are the person left coping with this, how do you deal with the reactions of other people? How do you tell other people without compounding your own pain? I have found a few things that helped me.

1) Choose whom you tell. It took me quite a long while to realise that not everybody needs to know. Even if you have had an emotional outburst in front of some acquaintance, shop assistant or unsuspecting member of the public, it is not necessary to explain it. If, like me, you feel the need to excuse yourself, it is useful to have a general phrase to hand, such as "Sorry, I have had some bad news recently", or "I'm dealing with some issues at the moment".

2) When friends and family start the "Why?" cycle, you can cut it short. Say something like, "I'd rather not talk about it, if you don't mind." You may have to say this several times. The trick is not to vary the phrase but just to keep repeating it in an even and pleasant tone. Then change the subject. Like this:

Great Aunt Maud: "Why would he want to break up such a lovely family?"

You: "I'd rather not talk about it, if you don't mind."

Great Aunt Maud: "Do you think he was jealous of your promotion?"

You: "I'd rather not talk about it, if you don't mind."

Great Aunt Maud "I always thought he had a hang-up about women working!"

You: "I'd rather not talk about it, if you don't mind. Isn't it lovely weather for the time of year?"

3) If all else fails, lie. Yes, I know, but you need to protect yourself too. (For those of sensitive conscience I have put a justification in brackets.) The point is that you don't *have* to listen to two hours of Great Aunt Maud telling you what a bounder she always thought he was, and a phrase like "I've got to go now" (well you *have* got to go or else you'll hit her), "I'm late for an appointment" (with the cat – you know she'll be waiting for some food), or "I think there's someone at the door" (this works well if you are on the phone, and you haven't actually said there *is* someone at the door) can save both of you a lot of anguish.

4) Find a phrase which describes your pain without keying into their lack of understanding, such as "I lost my husband". For example, one day when the children were spending the weekend with him and *her*, I took myself off to a creative arts workshop for the day. By coffee time my demeanour had obviously got too much for one acquaintance.

"You look really down; you haven't smiled all day," she said.

"I haven't got a lot to smile about," I replied. She didn't take the hint.

"But you're usually dancing around happily," she said.

"Yes, I know."

"Oh come on, cheer up!" she said. "It can't be that bad!"

"It is," I said simply.

"But this is a day for rejoicing!" she replied

I stopped at that point and just looked at her for a while. I didn't want to hit her. I didn't want to run out of the workshop and spend the day on my own. I didn't want to go into long explanations with a stranger. I didn't want to pretend everything was all right when it wasn't. What could I say that would justify my sadness and stop her questioning? Why did I have to justify anything anyway? I decided to hammer her with it verbally and see what happened. Very evenly, I said, "Six months ago I lost my husband and two children on the same day." She was horrified! Immediately sympathetic. Immediately apologetic. At last the questioning stopped. I was to be allowed my grief that day. There was one last, tentative, enquiry. "Was it... was it... a car crash?" she said.

"I'd rather not talk about it, if you don't mind," I said.

What's your reaction to that? Are you laughing? It really wasn't funny at the time. Are you shocked? Was I lying? Was I deceiving the poor woman? Or had I simply spoken a language she could understand? Would her reaction have been the same if I'd said I'd lost him to a 20-year-old with long, blonde hair? I would have been too ashamed to have said that anyway, terrified that she would have taken one look at me and thought "I'm not surprised!" There is a shame that attaches to separation and divorce that is not there when you lose a partner through bereavement. But the loss is the same. I had effectively communicated my loss to her.

I know a woman who went into work for six months after her husband had left and told no one. She felt the shame too acutely. There is a shame that attaches to separation and divorce. There is the underlying supposition that somehow, in some way, it must have been your fault. As we discussed in chapter three, you know now that if you have dealt with any justified guilt that might be yours you stand guiltless before God. You don't have to take delivery of the unjustified guilt. You have nothing to be ashamed of.

Finally:

5) DO find someone who does understand to talk to. Friend, counsellor, relative or priest, if they show an understanding (you'll know soon enough), treasure them! When you meet misunderstanding you can tell them about it, and they'll soon put it into perspective again. The number of times I've had my sanity restored, along with my faith in human nature, by friends with some real understanding of what I've been through. There are people – friends and professionals and groups – who do have an understanding. Search for those people, and hang on to them when you find them. People who understand can help bring closure, when you are ready.

Slowly I learned to establish my own boundaries, to choose whom I spoke to and what I said, and to refuse to accept the judgement that arose out of their ignorance. It is very hard to have to explain the pain as well as endure it. So don't. Unless you really feel up to it. Give them this book instead, with this section underlined(!), but be warned: they probably still won't get it.

Forgiveness

There is not a lot to say here. We covered it really in chapter three, didn't we? I've found that the only solution is to realise that some people will not understand because this type of pain or rejection or betrayal or ongoing trauma is beyond their experience. They simply do not understand it. They cannot understand it because they haven't experienced anything like it. The truth is really that we don't want them to understand, because we wouldn't wish that sort of pain on anyone. So the only thing we can do is establish boundaries that protect ourselves and, when people cross our boundaries, forgive them. They really don't know what they are doing. One of the root meanings of forgiveness is "to let go". We can take some practical steps to protect ourselves, as I've outlined above, but in the end when other people unintentionally or unknowingly hurt us all we can do is accept that they don't understand and let go of the resentment. Forgive them.

There *are* people who understand. At least, they have *an* understanding, but no two cases are alike. One thing I can say: God understands. He understands all the complexities of all the issues and he understands and loves *you*. In the end it is what HE thinks about us that matters, not what anyone else thinks. I take comfort and strength from the fact that I know he understands.

Chapter 5

Am I Going Mad?

It may have been that perceived lack of understanding that led to such a sense of isolation. Maybe it was the weariness and effort of carrying such a load for so long, just carrying on and on through never-ending greyness. Whatever the reason, a surprising two years after my husband had left I found myself clinically depressed. Not that I felt any sadder, just totally exhausted.

What is a broken heart?

The usual metaphor for grief is a broken heart – you know the picture: the carefully drawn heart shape neatly cracked down the middle with a clean zigzag line. This is a useful picture to an extent, but it really doesn't go far enough. It doesn't give any idea of the chaos going on inside.

I prefer to think of a broken heart as more like a broken machine. The machine may look the same as it always did, but it is not functioning properly any more. It is broken. I once had a clock/radio/alarm that developed a malfunction.

Imagine... Day after day, month after month, you've woken up to the gentle tones of Radio 2, Radio 4 or Gemini FM playing on your radio alarm clock. Each morning you hear: "Click. Beep beep beep beep BEEEEP,

the time is 7 o'clock and here are the news headlines...".
You open your eyes to see the red glow of the letters "7.00
am" and "Alarm 1" gently flashing. All is normal. All is
well. The day can proceed.

Then suddenly one day you are aroused by the
raucous noise: "Cock-a-doodle squawk! Cock-a-doodle
SQUAWK!" Oh, no! The kids have been playing with the
controls again and have tuned it to "Alternative alarm
sound 3 – the cockerel".

"Cock-a-doodle SQUAWK!" Your eyes are wide open
now and you watch in disbelief as the LCD display flashes
indiscriminate numbers that make no sense to your head
– 88888888 11:22 88888888 16:41 88888888 25:39. "Cock-
a-doodle SQUAWK" is *not* responding to the "Alarm off"
button and there is a smell of electrical burning in the air.
The machine is definitely malfunctioning. It's time to
pull the plug.

All that has happened is that the machine has
suffered from electrical overload, maybe due to an
outside power surge, maybe due to hidden damage or a
fault in its inner workings. We sometimes refer to people
as having a nervous breakdown due to emotional overload.

The electrician looks at your Super-Duper A1 Four-
Star Acme CD/Clock/Radio Alarm. It *looks* OK until he
takes the outer casing off to assess the damage. "Good!"
you think, "now he's going to mend it." Well, yes, and
there again... no. The first thing he does is start taking it
to bits. And then he spreads the bits out all over the
workbench. Your Super-Duper A1 Four-Star Acme CD/
Clock/Radio Alarm is now seriously gutted. Part of its
insides are blackened, some melted and stuck to others;
seared twisted bare wires contort back on each other.
Plastic coatings are melted. It is at this point that you
know your Super-Duper A1 Four-Star Acme CD/Clock/
Radio Alarm will never work again... but do not despair! It
is in the hands of an expert. The electrician smiles gently;

it's serious but he's seen this sort of thing plenty of times before; it's going to take time but once he's finished it'll be as good as new – better in fact if you'll allow him to put in the latest modifications, seeing as he's already got it apart.

There is another way machines tell us they are broken. The blank screen. You press the start button. Blank screen. You pull the plug out. Blank screen. You put the plug in and turn the switch on. Blank screen. You press everything in sight all at once – flicker – blank screen. In desperation you try the percussion method and hit it hard from above. No reaction. Now you are seriously worried. The machine is definitely broken.

In people it is sometimes labelled "emotional exhaustion". That report's due in today. So? You missed your turn on the duty rota. So? It's dinnertime, Mum. So? Are you getting up, Mum, it's gone one o'clock? So? Do you want to come out with us tonight? NO! And finally: I've written off your car/given you the sack/just heard your house has burnt down. So? The only reaction you get is a blank face.

Now you should really be worried – this person's heart (or spirit) is definitely broken. I think that it is this brokenness, this malfunctioning, that we call depression.

Depression is a killer

Depression is a killer. It kills by suicide. The trouble with my near-suicide experiences is that I didn't see them coming. I didn't consciously plan to end my life. It was not pre-meditated. It was just something that happened and then didn't happen. But I know it could have happened. I suppose there was just a long run up to it and then the circumstances were right. Like that storm I drove through that time (see chapter two) there was a time in my life when day after day after day was monotonous and grey. There was no enjoyment any more. I didn't feel dreadfully unhappy. In fact it was quite a relief that those storms of tears and extreme emotions had gone. In their place was a sort of weariness. A daily, ongoing weariness.

I didn't know that I was suicidal; I thought that if I was I'd be even *more* prone to angry or tearful outbursts than I had been. I just felt dead on the inside, and if you are dead on the inside you can't see much point in being alive on the outside. You might as well be dead on the outside too. Not that I ever vocalised that, or even really thought it. It just seemed to follow. I didn't feel sad any more, just extremely tired. I was tired of living. I didn't know that though, I just felt tired. Although my life was perfectly comfortable and secure there was no enjoyment in it. My friends thought I was getting better because I was no longer outwardly sad and angry and grieving. But there is a state of sadness too deep for tears. Lethargy, the inability to get on with life. Tiredness. Lack of interest. Hopelessness. These are the symptoms of depression.

I think I must have been in that sort of state of mind one day when I took a long walk in the dark alongside the river Dart. It was late and I was completely alone. I think I was just trying to walk away from the pain, but I carried it with me permanently. I couldn't remember when I hadn't. I walked along the edge of the quay wall and stood looking at the deep black water for a long while. It was winter. There was absolutely no one around. The only thought in my mind was how comforting it would be to sink under those rippling black waves and extinguish the pain.

Obviously I'm still here, so what stopped me? I'm not sure. I think it was a small quiet certainty somewhere deep that God wouldn't want it and would probably try to stop it. A lone fisherman would appear on the bank or a pleasure boat returning late! Angels come in many guises.

Oblivion appealed to me, but being wet and cold and rushed to hospital didn't. I let my footsteps take me to a neighbour's house instead. I stood on the doorstep and Tom opened the door. There was shock on his face when he saw me. He actually said, "You look like death; come in!" I didn't know it showed. He sat me by a roaring fire and held my hand while his wife pushed a glass of wine into my other hand and they asked gentle questions and listened until my heart softened enough to be able to cry again. In their sympathetic company the tears brought some relief. They kept telling me what an OK person I was. I didn't quite believe them, but some of it sank in. "But you've got a faith!" said Lorraine. "Your God will look after you." That made me smile. Two people of no specified belief telling me that I had to live for my God, who had a new life for me. Wasn't that supposed to be the other way around? It worked, though. Tom and Lorraine, did you know what you did for me that day? You do now. That night I went home to my bed instead of going back to the river.

When people *have* committed suicide I have heard others say, "How could they have been so selfish?" Surely it must have been *obvious* to the suicidal person that they would be missed and others would be traumatised if they died? However I suspect that it would never even have occurred to them that anyone would mind if they died. Or miss them if they were no longer there. I actually got to the point where it seemed that everyone would actually be better off without me. I suppose that is called low self-esteem. I didn't know that at the time. It just seemed *obvious* that they would be happier if I wasn't there. Or maybe in their minds at the time there was no thought of other people at all. There was probably no thought of anything. Just greyness and pain. An incurable emotional ache that never goes away. It's not even worth acknowledging. If you do you'll only have a storm of emotions again, and that would be too exhausting . You just don't have the strength for it.

Healing

Broken hearts need repair. Personally I hate the phrase "time is the great healer", as I didn't find that time healed anything. Doctors heal; it's their job and they have expertise. God heals; he knows better than any human person what is wrong and what needs to be done about it, and the love of friends and family is healing. These things, over time, can heal if you have access to them, but it is not time itself that heals. However, it does *take* time to heal, and serious damage can take a long time to heal and might need many different approaches: rest, medication, prayer and the love and support of friends.

Emotional pain is real but unseen. We often don't recognise it, even in ourselves, until the results of it manifest themselves in our senses. "He broke down in tears at work!" "Doctor, I've got palpitations/headaches/ no energy." Physical symptoms are often the first clue to emotional pain. Depression is part of the cycle of emotions that rage intermittently, as described in chapter two. It is a feeling that comes and thankfully goes again. I was used to that, but after two years I was surprised to find that I hit a long season of depression. It was as though I had run out of emotional energy. I went to the doctor and took time off work. I was convinced that a few weeks' rest would put me right. The weeks turned into months, and I still felt no better. My diary entries of the time speak for themselves.

Nov. 10

"I see no future. I see no answer. God is intangible. Invisible. I know no companionship. No tenderness. No intimacy. No one's interest. I feel isolated, marginalised, unwanted, and

useless. Increasingly I lose the old but I don't see anything new. Has it always been like this? People say you'll learn from this. Well, I'm learning that's for sure! I'm learning about loneliness, broken-heartedness and hopelessness."

Nov. 13
"I WISH THIS SEASON WERE OVER."

Dec. 10
"Life feels very heavy. I don't know whether I'm coming or going. The solicitors are demanding a response to their letter within a fortnight and I can't even open the letter, let alone decide what to do. I feel horribly alone. I feel ill and I need someone to look after me but there is no one, so I have to look after myself. Everything is an effort and I can't remember when it was different. I cannot imagine any brightness in the future, only grey dullness, and I have forgotten what happiness is. I see it on the faces of other people but it looks fake. I call for God but he doesn't seem to hear."

At that point my diary entries stopped for seven months. That is probably because my brain stopped. I wasn't any sadder than I had been before. I wasn't crying all the time like I had been before. It's just that my brain refused to process more than one thought at a time. Literally.

I remember walking into the village one Saturday morning to buy eggs, milk and bread from the corner shop. No chance! I got to the shop and bought bread but the other two items had fled my brain by then. I tried to recall them but got nothing in my head but a blank screen. I knew there was something else to buy so I bought apples. They were in front of me. I walked back home and opened the fridge to make lunch. Then I discovered that I had no eggs or milk. I set off the short distance for the shop again, confident that I could remember TWO items! I was wrong.

On my *third* visit to the shop that morning I met a neighbour. Both bemused and amused, I related my morning's excursions. Her reaction was beautifully enlightening and very kind: "So you really are depressed, then," she said matter-of-factly. "Am I?" I said. "But I don't feel sad!" Then she explained to me that clinical depression was characterised by feelings of tiredness, loss of memory and the inability to settle to anything. Having trouble sleeping or taking little interest in life and sleeping too much can also be symptoms of depression. She then went on to tell me that it could be very easily and quickly treated with the latest modern drugs.

At first her matter-of-factness offended me, but very soon I realised she was just accepting depression as another one of those illnesses that we can diagnose and treat. If you have diabetes you take insulin to rebalance your chemical levels, and if you have depression you can take fluoxetine to help rebalance your chemical levels. I had resisted taking drugs somehow, seeing it as a failure and, I think, worried that Prozac would just make me "high" as a sort of escape from the depression. Actually that's not how fluoxetine or other SSRIs (see below) work. We don't understand it all fully, but basically the balance of chemicals in our body determines mood. Stress produces adrenaline, also called epinephrine, which helps us in emergencies. It does this by quickly mopping up as much serotonin as it can. Serotonin regulates the balance of hormones in our bodies so that we feel content and "normal". It is no use feeling relaxed and normally content when a rhinoceros is charging you. You don't want to stop and appreciate the beautiful colours of the daisies either; you just need to move FAST to get out of the way of that charging animal and preserve your life! Adrenalin tells the body "RUN! NOW!" and gives it the surge of energy to do so. So stress produces adrenaline, and adrenaline suppresses serotonin.

SSRIs are Selective Serotonin Reuptake Inhibitors. That means they stop the body from reabsorbing the serotonin it makes. So the chemical levels slowly rebalance themselves. I had lived in a state of extreme stress for two years, never knowing what emotion was going to hit me next. I remember feeling that I wanted to be happy, but I couldn't. I mean *couldn't*. I was sometimes in situations that were making me happy, but I was unable to feel it. It was like wanting to walk but finding that your legs won't respond. I tried, but I couldn't feel happy. I believe now that I didn't have enough chemicals to be happy with, but I'm no doctor or scientist and can only explain how it felt to me on the inside. After a month on medication, I felt no different. I presumed the chemicals were not working, but they were. Slowly and imperceptibly they were allowing my natural levels of serotonin to re-establish themselves. I didn't know this at the time; I only knew that one day I woke up in bed feeling warm and snug. It was such a surprise! Like recognising an old friend. "I remember feeling like this before!" I thought to myself. "A long time ago." From then on I knew I was getting better, and my feelings of contentment began to return. This sort of antidepressant did not make me feel "high" at all, just normal. After a while the doses are gradually reduced and your body takes over the job of balancing itself as usual.

Depression is an emotional reaction to the circumstances we find ourselves in. It is the right reaction to very painful circumstances. It is the correct and natural reaction. It therefore follows that the depression will never entirely lift until you deal with the underlying causes of the pain. That's where talking can be so useful. It helps you see what's going on. It helps you analyse it and put it into some order. Somehow just acknowledging the problem can deprive it of its power. It helps you come to terms with what has happened. Often you cannot change the circumstances, but you can change the way you react to them. It helps you see a way forward or ways of coping with new stressful situations when they arise. I was very lucky in having a counsellor recommended by my doctor and in having many friends who listened to me and many more who prayed. I needed them all before I could come to terms with my loss and start building a new life. It takes some courage to accept this sort of help. I was terrified of being labelled "mad" or emotionally unstable, but it really is more courageous to face up to the pain than to carry on as if it isn't there. As a friend once said to me, if you were in a road accident you wouldn't refuse intensive care, operations to set bones or physiotherapy. There is no need to refuse professional help in an emotional life accident either.

God, the Saviour

I have come to see that when God calls himself Saviour he is not referring to just one act performed for all two thousand years ago. That was merely the extreme example of how far he is prepared to go in saving us. Like the psalmist, I experienced God as my Saviour in my everyday life. Mostly in the form of people turning up when I most needed them. Sometimes in an overwhelming sense of his presence.

By definition, someone who needs to be saved cannot help themselves. They are in a life-or-death situation that is beyond their control. Sometimes they can call for help; sometimes they cannot. This makes no difference to the lifeguard on the beach; if he sees someone in danger he goes to their rescue. God is like that. He acts independently to protect us and rescue us.

Being saved is a vulnerable position. You feel so

helpless. That's because you *are* so helpless. However the experience of being rescued adds security to life. There is much in this whole process that is beyond my power to deal with, but there is nothing that is beyond his power. He is always there, unseen and unfelt maybe, but always there. If he is prepared to be my Saviour, and he says he is, then I am always secure, even when the waves overwhelm me. "When you go through deep waters and great trouble, I will be with you. When you go through rivers of difficulty, you will not drown!" (Isaiah 43:2). "Though I walk through the valley of the shadow of death, I will fear no evil, for you are with me" (Psalm 23:4, NIV). "He lifted me out of the pit of despair, out from the bog and the mire, and set my feet on a hard firm path and steadied me as I walked along" (Psalm 40:2). I was conscious of God saving me on many days, in many ways.

"Christians shouldn't suffer emotional pain"

There are some in the church today who think we should never be sad or depressed. They seem to think that having the victory means being happy all the time. This is not borne out by the Bible or by experience. Romans 12:15 (NIV) says, "Rejoice with those who rejoice; mourn with those who mourn," and in 2 Corinthians 1:3–5 (NIV) Paul writes, "Praise be to the God and Father of our Lord Jesus Christ, the Father of compassion and the God of all comfort, who comforts us in all our troubles, so that we can comfort those in any trouble with the comfort we ourselves have received from God. For just as the sufferings of Christ flow over into our lives, so also through Christ our comfort overflows." If we are not in distress we don't need to be comforted. If we *are* in distress, one of the wonders of our God is that he can reach into our lives with his comfort.

One of the strengths of Christianity as against all

other religions is the belief in the Incarnation, the idea that God became a human being and experienced in our reality all that we go through. Jesus knew what it was like to be under extreme stress and at the end of his emotional strength. In Gethsemane, Jesus knew he was going to suffer and die. He taught that to his students/disciples on numerous occasions, one of which is recorded in John 12:27. It is the last week of his life, and he has just said, "Whoever loves his own life will lose it, whoever hates his own life in this world will keep it for life eternal" (John 12:25, TEV), using a seed as an illustration: the wheat seed is buried in the ground and dies, but out of its death comes a whole ear of corn and many more seeds. Jesus never taught anything that he wasn't prepared to do himself. That doesn't mean it was easier for him, and the next passage gives away something of the strain he was under as a human being. "Now my heart is troubled – and what shall I say? Shall I say, 'Father, do not let this hour come upon me?' But that is why I came – so that I might go through this hour of suffering. Father, bring glory to your name!"

There we have it, a very real human dilemma – the realisation of what was coming, the dread of it and the choice again to go with the plans of his Father. No wonder his heart – his emotions – became troubled. Jesus knew how he was going to die (verses 32–33) and I think this is a moment when the horror of it overwhelmed him. The loneliness of this place must have been emotionally awful. His closest and best-taught friends did not understand what he was doing (even Peter had said, "This shall never happen to you!" [Matthew 16:22, NIV]). The best theologians of the time were convinced that God would always protect the Messiah. The people quoted the Scripture back at him (John 12:34), the accepted doctrine *"The messiah will live forever!"* (TEV). They just didn't understand. If this man were really anointed he wouldn't be facing suffering; God would protect his life from all evil people. That was the orthodox doctrine. Jesus knew better. He'd already faced this before he started his ministry. In the temptations (Matthew 4:1–11) Jesus had already abandoned the right to the supernatural protection promised in Psalm 91:11–12, which offered him angels to protect him even from a stubbed toe! He preferred to leave the decisions about his personal protection to God.

What do we do in Gethsemane?

Matthew's account of Jesus in Gethsemane shows a man at the end of his emotional resources. You know the story: Jesus goes up to Jerusalem knowing that arrest, torture and death by crucifixion are waiting for him there (Matthew 20:17–19). He spends a week going from one violent emotion to another. The joy of Palm Sunday, the anger of the cleansing of the Temple, heart-stopping public arguments with some of the most powerful people in the capital where a false move could result in arrest, death and riot not just for him but for the friends and innocent bystanders around him. Tests of mental agility that require every ounce of his extensive biblical knowledge and debating skills along with reliance on the wisdom of his Father, played out against the agonising awareness that the very scholars who ought to understand who he is and why he has come to them are blind to the truth. An awareness that leads to the outcry of righteous anger reported in Matthew 23.

Here you can see the agony of a prophet who knows he has to warn his leaders of the truth and consequences of their behaviour despite the consequences for his own personal safety. Agony that pours out in a very public display of grief that overflows simply at the sight of Jerusalem. Knowing that there is a price on his head, arrangements for the Last Supper have to be made secretly and he isn't even sure if he'll make it to that meal.

During the meal Jesus faced up to the emotional reality that betrayal was coming not from one of his worst enemies but from one of his closest friends. He tried to explain again to incredulous friends, who still didn't get it, what was about to happen, this time using the symbols of bread and wine on the table in front of them. He was worried for his friends and took time to give personal words of strengthening and warning to them. Even then, on the way to Gethsemane (now a synonym for agony, then just one of the camping sites around the city at festival time), Luke reports an argument amongst the party as to who was the greatest, underlining the fact that they were in the last hours of their time with Jesus and they still hadn't understood the basics of his teaching. I don't know what that does to someone's sense of their own self-esteem and the "success" of their ministry, or what reserves of self-control it needed to respond to such an argument so patiently when time was so short (Luke 22:24–30).

So how did the holy Son of God, who never sinned, respond to such extremes of mental and emotional pressure? Look at Matthew 26:36–46. The first thing he did was take himself away from the majority of the party, because they were simply unable to understand what he was going through. *"Sit here while I go over there and pray,"* he said, at once reassuring them and distancing himself from them. He took only his three closest friends with him, Peter, James and John, and he allowed them to see the state of his heart. The Good News version says, *"Grief and anguish came over him."* Strong words. One translation of the Greek here is "deeply depressed". Jesus was overwhelmed by grief and deeply depressed. It was the correct response to such mental pressure in his life. Finally he could tell his closest friends what was really going on inside him. *"My soul is overwhelmed with sorrow to the point of death,"* he said. Jesus hadn't experienced physical torture at this point. This was emotional pain that was killing him.

Maybe you know something of what that feels like. I do. I'm not saying that I have had anything like the pressure that Jesus was suffering from; I'm saying that I've been pushed beyond my emotional limits to the point at which I thought the pain would kill me. I've been in a place where the weight of that pain was unbearable and I thought I would die from it. It was a place where physical death would have been welcome as a release from the emotional agony. If you are dead on the inside, death on the outside just seems like a rationalisation. Few understand this. It was when I was in such a place that God drew my attention to this verse to show me that *he* did.

Did Jesus see on the faces of his friends the same feelings that I've seen of the faces of my friends? Profound sympathy, mixed with an inability to grasp what's really going on inside you (no one can), and a subdued panic caused by searching impotently for something, anything, that will make it better for you. Not knowing how to respond, not daring to respond for fear of getting it wrong. It's at this point that Jesus himself tells them what he needs: *"Stay here and keep watch with me."* Stay with me. Don't say anything. Don't do anything. Just stay with me. It helps. It really helps. You see, at this point there is nothing even your closest friends can do. This is a private agony and the only one who can help is God. *"Going a little farther, he fell with his face to the ground and prayed."* Jesus left even his closest human companions to throw himself into the arms of his God. I find the NIV's translation *"fell"* is telling. There comes a point when emotional pain prevents the body from functioning. Here it seems that Jesus was truly prostrate with grief. At that point there is nothing left to do but pray. His prayer was not long. "I don't want to do this, but if there is no other way... (*Surely* there's some other way!)." "If it's what you want, I will."

And then God gave him the strength to carry on. Luke's gospel (chapter 22:43) tells us that an angel from heaven came to him, strengthening him in spirit. That was what he needed, and although he was in an "agony of mind" he had the strength to continue to pray and to get up and face what was to come. So Jesus needed supernatural help at this point to enable him to continue. He really was at the end of his own emotional resources. It is certainly true that God himself knows every stress and strain of the darkest experiences we go through. That's why he has the ability and the right to support and heal us. Cling to him. He knows what it is like. Amazing God!

Chapter 6

Have You Got a Wall I Could Demolish?

After the deadness of depression was over I found that the first emotion to emerge was anger. I was angry with my husband, of course. So angry that I sometimes felt murderous. I didn't know I was capable of such an emotion. I do now. I was angry that he seemed to have everything working out the way HE wanted it. I didn't often give vent to my anger on paper, but there is one diary entry that is quite specific in its vituperation. I can't quote it here – they'd never print it. It's probably enough to say that "fornicating", "manipulating", "devious" and "arrogant" were some of the milder adjectives I used, and there right in the middle of it was the heartfelt appeal: "Why can't you just do the decent thing and *die*?" From my point of view it seemed as if it all would have been so much easier to bear if only he had died. That I suppose is at the heart of crimes of passion and all murderous intent. Oh yes, it was certainly there in my heart at times, I was so angry with him! Other diary entries I *can* quote verbatim.

I was angry about the endlessness of the ongoing situation:

> *I am so angry. So angry. So angry! I don't know what to do with it or where to put it or who to turn to for help. Angry! I am so fed up with the endlessness of it all. Variation upon variation of twisting the knife and I'm just supposed to put up with it all while Mr Innocent comes up smelling of roses.*

I don't like this fire! I don't like this storm! Earlier today I read Isaiah and came to this:

"Woe to those who call evil good and good evil, who put darkness for light and light for darkness, who put bitter for sweet and sweet for bitter! Woe to those who are wise in their own eyes and prudent and shrewd in their own sight. Woe to those who are mighty heroes at drinking wine, men of strength at mixing alcoholic drinks!"

The quote is in chapter 5:20–22, and it obviously struck a chord that day. Anger is not a comfortable emotion, though. I also wrote that it felt as if my heart were being ploughed with spikes.

As well as being angry with my husband and with the ongoing situation as a whole, I was angry with other people. One evening I wrote:

I hate wearing masks, but they've become essential! My children don't want to see me in tears all the while. They want Mummy to be happy, so I mask it. My class need me to be in control. They are at a loss if I am perplexed or angry, tired, sad or at my wits' end, so I mask it. My friends want me to be better. They don't want to hear an endless story of pain; they can't bear it. So I smile and say I'm fine. The people in church don't want their marriages threatened. If it can happen to me it can happen to them, you see. They don't want God to let them down. They are afraid, so I have to pretend. "At least you have God with you," they say, and their smile is self-satisfied and I close my mouth, suppress my emotions, raise my mask and return to a life alone. The coffee cup is where I left it, the bed unmade, the bills unopened, everything frozen just as it was when I walked out of the door that morning. The house is huge and echoing around me. Everything I do reminds me that he is not there. Everything I pass we built or made together. No one asks how I am. No one smiles to see me. No one's there.

The house echoes with silence. My religious friends rest secure and content in the knowledge that I am never alone. God is with me. I open my eyes. I see nothing. I listen and listen and hear only the anguish of my heart. I long for an arm around my shoulders but all I feel is the dead weight of grief in my bones. I reach for a hand and find empty air. This is cold comfort. This is Job's comfort. "Express your feelings," they say. They couldn't take it if I did!

What's more, I found I began to get angry with *all* men. I was worried when I saw it happening. This attitude was summed up in the banter of some divorcées I had met. "Men! Who needs them? They're only good for one thing!" and the bitterness showed on their faces through the raucous laughter. I didn't want to be like that! I really didn't want to be like that. Such anger! And I never knew when it was going to erupt!

Results of anger

I slowly began to realise that if I didn't find a way of handling the anger there could be some dire consequences for me.

- It could grow to overwhelm me one day and lead me into some action that I would regret. I never actually contemplated murder, but I know some people who have. I can understand why. The ongoing pain is so bad that it seems as if it would be very much easier if the other partner just wasn't there.
- If it stayed in my system it could fester and transmute itself into bitterness and resentment, which would mar my life and my personality. I really did not want to become like those bitter divorcées. I had seen parents whose constantly expressed resentment had poisoned the minds of their children against the

other parent. I didn't want to be responsible for that either. Besides, half of the people in the world belong to the opposite sex. Men! There was no way I could get away from them! I couldn't spend the rest of my life being resentful of and making snide remarks about 49% of the world's population! What's more, they were my colleagues; they were married to my friends; they were people I was responsible for at work and, for goodness' sake, two of them were my own sons! I didn't care if I never had an intimate relationship with a man again – such a thing looked like a complete impossibility at the time anyway – but I knew that I was going to have to relate in *some* way to men for the rest of my life.

- I had read somewhere that depression could be caused by internalised anger. I could see that tendency starting in me. My anger at being unable to control the awful situation I was in was turning into helplessness, which led to hopelessness and increased depression.

- There is also the question of what part repressed anger might play in making illnesses worse. As we come to see that we are whole people, not bodies separated from minds and emotions, we have an increasing understanding that anger is not good for our physical health either.

Altogether it was not a good prospect to contemplate! In fact the more I contemplated it, the more angry I got! On top of everything else he'd now left me all THIS to deal with! That made me furious! I realised then that I had a problem.

Biblical perspectives on anger

There's nothing wrong with being angry. Of all the emotions, it seems that people in general and Christians in particular seem to have a problem accepting that they or other people are angry. We seem to think it is wrong. The key verse here is Ephesians 4:26, which says *"Be angry, but do not sin,"* or, in some translations, *"In your anger do not sin."* In other words it's OK to *be* angry but not to let it lead you into doing something wrong.

Why would God make us with this emotion if he didn't want us to have it? What's it for? Jesus was angry when he drove the traders out of the Temple with a whip (John 2:15). We prefer to think that he wasn't. We try to protect God from the accusation of having a "wrong" emotion by calling it "righteous indignation". This is anger for a right reason. In Mark 11:16 it says that he wouldn't allow anyone to carry household equipment through the Temple area (they were using it as a short cut), so this wasn't just an uncontrolled burst of fury. It took time and sustained effort. This was anger for a right reason. The reason Jesus gives himself, by quoting Isaiah 56:7 and Jeremiah 7:11, is that the Temple was meant to be a house of prayer, not a den of robbers! It is right to be angry about wrongdoing and unfairness. Someone's anger may be a signal that you have stepped over their boundaries, stepped over the line or, in old English, "trespassed", which is another word for sinned. The prophets are full of expressed anger which shows the people of the world that they have crossed God's boundaries. It is true that God does not treat us as we deserve, but from time to time he shows us exactly where the boundaries are.

Religious hypocrisy seemed to make Jesus angrier than anything else. Read Matthew 23. It is an account of a stinging diatribe against the religious leaders in

Jerusalem. I don't believe we'd think very highly of a young man who stood in Canterbury Cathedral and publicly screamed that the Archbishop of Canterbury and the officials of the cathedral were blind fools, hypocrites and internally filthy (not that I am suggesting they are!), and then followed it up with some choice words, which I think lose something in the translation: "You snakes, you brood of vipers, how will you escape going to hell?" I'm not an expert in New-Testament Greek or first-century Aramaic, but that sounds rude to me. The issue that was behind this anger is in verse 13 (NIV): "You shut the kingdom of heaven in men's faces!" Religious teachers were supposed to make the things of God clear to the people, not use the position for their own advancement or make it *more* difficult for ordinary people to find God!

Jesus shouted at the religious leaders, but he didn't hit them. He scattered the moneychangers' coins, but he didn't steal them. He drove out the sheep, he didn't maim them; the doves went flying, he didn't wring their necks. And I daresay all the traders were there the next day pursuing their business as usual, so he didn't even ruin their trade. He was angry and he showed it, but he didn't sin.

So, how can I express the anger I rightly feel without hurting anyone?

What do you do with the feeling?

Even when you have sorted out all that you possibly can, as amicably as you possibly can, there will still be a residue of hurt and there is bound to be a residue of anger. Anger seems to be the most difficult emotion to express. Here are some strategies that I have found useful.

Express it verbally

- Tell a friend. You have to pick the right friend. One who will listen without judgement. I told my counsellor, Amanda.
- Tell God exactly how angry you are. God is always there. Rant and rave at him – he can take it. He knows what you are thinking anyway. He loves you anyway. He won't zap you. He didn't zap me. Mind you, there were times when I was so angry I wouldn't have minded if he had! God is so much bigger than we are. I often think of him as being like a parent, with me as the toddler hammering on his knee. He can take it. My son used to get SO angry when he couldn't get the round peg into the square hole in his posting box, and then he got even MORE angry when *I* couldn't do it for him! I couldn't explain to him why it was impossible, but I understood his frustration.
- Tell your diary. Write it all down: you can always tear it up again later, but it helps to get it out.
- If you have difficulty expressing anger verbally, let the Psalms do it for you. Read them aloud. Read them with feeling: you're allowed to do that; it's Scripture! Psalms 35, 52, 53, 55, 58, 59 and 69 are good for starters!

Remember, you are doing this for YOU. Somehow when you acknowledge a feeling it loses its power. It's out in the open. When the anger is expressed it loses some of its power and then it doesn't overwhelm you or fester.

Express it physically

I don't suggest that you take a baseball bat to his more delicate parts, or a left hook to her smiling face (not that either has ever crossed my mind), but some form of harmless physical expression is good. I once stormed around the village until I met an acquaintance who was renovating their house, and I asked if they had a wall to demolish. I am not a big person but I think I could have had the job finished in ten minutes that day! Other more accessible ways of expressing anger are playing squash, jogging hard, using the punch bag at the gym, going to the top of the hill and screaming at the top of your voice and, an oldie but a goldie, smashing crockery on the kitchen floor or garden path. The latter is especially good if you never liked that crockery anyway.

Like all the emotions, anger is one that comes (and goes) at any time in this process of recovery, but I had a time when it was the predominant feeling. It frightened me a little, because I couldn't always control it. You don't want to be driving a car in a state like that! I think God must have had an angel on the front seat of my car on more than one occasion. Or maybe the angel was in the guise of the little old lady driving that Lada at some ridiculously slow speed on the road in front of me. I'd storm and mutter and rage sarcastically and she'd keep plodding steadily on in the middle of the road with me stuck behind her, until I realised that revving up to hit 80mph in a built-up area had probably never been a good idea and that the little old lady was keeping to the legal speed limit. Well, nearly.

The thing is, you get taken by surprise. You've had a perfectly good day; all is calm on the western front, and then something happens out of the blue. The phone rings and the kids have decided that they won't be coming over that day after all, or the boiler's gone wrong again and he always used to fix it. Suddenly you are in a rage! In *The Waltons* this is the point where John Boy would go out to the woodpile and chop wood. I went to the bottle bank. It was an inspired idea from one of my most sensible friends. She drove up one day with her car boot FULL of empty bottles and glass jars. "I've been thinking," she said. "Pummelling a pillow is not good enough, is it? This should keep you going for a bit." I have such good friends. I worked my way through that pile and all the others she saved for me, storming up to the other end of the village with as much as I could carry, bags in each hand, and then not just posting them but *chucking* them through the holes in the bottle bank with as much force as possible, relishing the smashing sound and muttering obscenities as they went. She was right. It was very satisfying. It got the anger out of my system, and by the time I'd walked back home it had cleared the air quite a bit. I still have a tendency to save my empty bottles until they overflow from the cupboard. You never know when you might need them.

God's creative solutions

What I have described are ways of dealing with the symptoms of anger. The symptoms will continue as long as there is a cause. The cause needs to be dealt with. If you can work out exactly what it is that you are angry about, what it is that is unfair in this situation, you might be able to deal with it directly. If the financial arrangements are unfair, then take steps to make that known and deal with it. You don't just have to put up with it. Sometimes it is possible to sort it out. The Bible's advice is to take a friend and express the perceived injustice to the one who has wronged you and see if you can come to an agreement about it. In the matter of divorce settlements that's what mediators and your legal people are there for. You don't need to be walked over. Some injustices are put right that way and thus the cause of the anger is removed.

However, as we all know, even with the best legal people in the world, many injustices simply aren't put right. That's true in all areas of life. Divorce settlements are no exception. What's more, some things just *can't* be sorted out that way. For example, if you both want the dog, you can't both have it, so one of you is going to feel angry about it. In these last two cases there is nothing for it but to revert to God's antidote – forgiveness. You feel angry: that is the signal that you have been wronged. You try to get the wrong put right. If that is not possible, you forgive; that releases you from the feeling and releases it to God, then the anger goes.

But what do you do with the things you just can't forgive? There *are* some things you just can't forgive. They go too deep; they are too wide-ranging and they hurt far too much. When I hit those places I didn't even try. I just cried. The particular hurt will be different for different people. The issue is irrelevant. The point is that one night I felt the extent of the pain of my hurt in a certain area and saw the ramifications of it, and I *couldn't* forgive. (If you are reading this and you don't understand that, you are a very lucky person.) The results of that were immediate. I began to hate him. I couldn't believe that he could be *that* cruel to me. I couldn't believe that a person could be so cruel to another person! I couldn't believe that a man could be so cruel to a woman. Then, in hating him, I found I was hating all men. Hate leads on to hate. A heart closed against him was closed against all men. I don't know the psychological process that lies behind that. I suppose that my husband had come to define "men" for me. So in hating him I was rejecting him, and in rejecting him I was rejecting all men. How could I ever trust another man again? Especially if they claimed to be "Christian"?

Be prepared for God's creative solutions in your life. I had enough problems to deal with. I didn't want to become an embittered man-hater on top of it all. I could see that was the road I was going down. Tracing it back, I saw that this attitude to men stemmed from the resentment I was feeling towards men in general, which came from the hatred I felt towards one particular man because of the hurt he had done me, which I was unable to forgive. It all came back to forgiveness, letting go of the hurt.

I didn't share this with anyone because I didn't want to be told to forgive what I knew I couldn't forgive, thus adding more guilt to the pile I was already carrying. I didn't want to be told to forgive my husband and pray for him every time it came into my mind. I didn't want to be told what I already knew, that forgiveness is a matter of the will not the feelings and that Jesus told us to love our enemies and forgive those who have despitefully used us! This pain was too much. I *couldn't* forgive. I did share it with God because he reads my mind anyway, and if he were going to zap me he would have done it long ago. I've never seen the point of trying to pretend to God. Then I realised that even God had come to earth as a *man*! Was I going to write *him* off as well, or make Jesus an exception to the rule? This was getting more complicated by the minute and I had no answer to it. I resorted to prayer. "Help!" I said, and meant it. The sour faces of those women I'd met kept coming back to me, and I really did not want to be like that. It was an entirely selfish prayer.

What came into my mind then was my solicitor waving his hand at the two filing cabinets in the corner of his office. "I've hundreds of cases in there of people trying to get as much access to their children as you've already got," he said – not entirely sympathetically, I thought at the time. "They're mostly men, of course." This memory kept coming back to me over the next few days and I couldn't work out why.

Then I was in a restaurant and overheard a total stranger pouring his heart out to his friend about how he'd come home from a long tour of duty with the army to find his wife living in their house with another man. His main complaint was that she wouldn't let him see their little girl. Suddenly my mind began to clear. There were *men* out there hurting as much as I was! There were *men* separated from day-to-day contact with their children through the actions of their wives. There were *men* who were finding it difficult to see any good in any women because of the damage done to them by one woman!

Then, in class, teaching the kids about marriage and divorce (I have often thought it would have been a lot easier if I had been a geography teacher), a list of statistics hit me. One in three marriages ends in divorce and figures among those professing a Christian faith are no lower than the norm. (By the way, that also means that 66% of marriages last a lifetime – just thought I'd mention it.)

Slowly it dawned on me that there were *Christian men* out there hurting as much as I was because of what women had done to them! Men who maybe shied away from women and never wanted to speak to them again. Men who maybe would sneer at *me* because of what I represented: woman. "But that would be unfair," I protested. "I haven't done anything to them!" "Quite," said God.

It set me thinking. My mind crystallised on one hypothetical man. I didn't know any such men locally, so I imagined him living somewhere a little further afield in the west country, maybe in Cornwall or up the motorway a bit, somewhere towards Bristol. If he had young children I knew that he would lose the right to live with them even if it had been *her* betrayal or her choice to leave. The courts generally support the status quo for the sake of the children and the status quo is usually that the mother has primary care of young children. Even if they were boys. I imagined that he had lost two boys as I had lost two girls. In that case he had most likely lost his home, too. I thought of the separated men I had known in the past, forced out of the family home they had put so much effort into, left to live in rented rooms by themselves, yet paying the bills on the family home. I thought of the man in the café… she might even have moved *her* lover into the family home!

"OK," I said to God. "So there are men out there hurt by women. But still don't ask me to pray for my husband when I feel this pain – it hurts too much; I can't do it."

"Then pray for the man," said God. It was a masterly plan.

Every time I felt the dreadful pain of what man can do to woman and felt tempted to write off the whole of *man*kind, I would think of this one man, living in his rented rooms, apart from his family because of what one woman had done to him. And I would pray for him. Mind you, I wasn't into an academic or psychological exercise. I said to God, if I'm going to be praying I'd better be praying for a real man, not just some imaginary exercise in spiritual psychiatry.

"I want you to choose me a real man who will actually benefit from these prayers," I said. "And as he's a real man we'd better stop calling him just 'the man' and dignify him with a name. What shall we call him?"

"How about 'Chris'?" said God.

"Good idea!" I said, for, after all, he was a Christian. "Is that Kris with a 'K' as in Kristian, or Chris with a 'C' as in Christopher – Christ-bearer?"

"Chris as in Christopher," said God. So that's what we called him.

"There's just one more thing," I said, knowing I was entering into quite a deal here and not wanting the effort to go to waste. "I'd like to meet that man one day, and when I do I'd like to know it's him."

"OK," said God.

So that's how it started.

Every time I hit the unbearable pain, the awful anger, the depth of hurt that I couldn't forgive, I'd forgive my ex-husband, "my man", as a matter of will and then I'd

PRAY for "the man" who had been similarly hurt by a woman. Pouring my feminine blessings into his wounds. After all, I knew something of what it really felt like to be rejected, to lose those you loved. At holiday times, when arrangements with my kids were so difficult, I'd pray that *his* arrangements would be smoothed out, that he'd be able to see his children, and that, even if it was only a short time they had together, it would be a *good* time. I prayed that they'd grow up knowing he loved them and that he'd really know that he was loved by them. After a difficult day at work, coming home to an empty house, the washing up and the impossibility of cooking for myself, I'd feel the pain and note the anger and resentment rising and I'd pray for him. At night going to an empty bed, alone, bereft and rejected, I'd pray for the man who might be feeling the same way. "Look after 'the man' God," I'd say. "Let him know you are with him; bless him, bless Chris, wherever he is tonight. Give him a good night's sleep." It was God's strategy, and it worked for me. I've come out of this without a huge resentment against men. Praise God! He'll have a different strategy for you. You'll have a different problem; he'll have a different answer. It'll be for you specifically, so look out for it. He's very creative.

Oh and just in case you were wondering, one day several years later, at a west country Christian conference in Exeter, I met a man, a complete stranger. We bumped into each other in the foyer and got into conversation and, as we were talking, at the back of my mind, in the gentlest of still small voices, I heard God whisper, "It's him." But that's another story.

Chapter 7

Who Am I?

I think that a lot of my depression and anger were because I no longer knew who I was. It wasn't just my world that fragmented when my husband left, it was myself. My husband told me he was definitely leaving the day before I was due to go to a week's Christian conference in the summer of 1997. "We'll discuss the practicalities with the children when you get back," he said. I didn't sleep that night. I arrived at that conference – I had nowhere else to go – in a state of extreme psychological fragmentation. It was a curious internal landscape to survey. I had never known anything like it. I felt as fragile as a shattered vase the moment before it breaks into a thousand pieces. I could barely relate to anyone. I could not understand how I was still walking. I didn't know who I was any more. My self-image was so tied up with him and the family. My picture of myself had always included him, and so it should have. We two were one. To see me was in some way to see him as well, or the reflection of him in me. I was wife to a lovely man and mother to four children.

Then in a day I was neither wife nor single person. I was married but with none of the advantages. I was suddenly a full-time mother to two children and a part-time mother to two children. How can you be a part-time mother? I didn't know how to function in these roles. I hadn't had any practice. I wasn't prepared for it, and I didn't choose it. In the sudden loss of my husband, I shared the problems of a bereaved wife.

However, I had a deeper problem. Even in their

deepest grief, most bereaved people know that their loved one did not choose to leave. I knew that mine did. What did that say about me? What did it do to my self-worth? At a recent funeral I heard the bereaved wife say, "I always knew I was his treasure." It really touched me. I cried for her grievous loss, but I also cried for myself because I saw in that one phrase that in losing her husband she had not lost her self-worth, whereas I had. She knew she had been prized, valued, appreciated and treasured. I knew I had been scorned, despised, criticised and rejected. She was grieving, but she was honoured by others and had respect for herself. I was grieving, but I was regarded with suspicion by others and felt ashamed of myself.

As we have already discussed in chapter three, you feel guilt when you believe you have done something wrong. It is to do with actions. Shame is to do with who you *are*. It shows you believe you are a worthless person. It is extraordinarily difficult to value yourself highly when the person who knows you best puts your value at nothing. My husband was not excessively nasty to me, but he made it quite clear that he wanted nothing at all to do with me. I was of no value to him. Yet he knew me better than anyone. He had known me longer than anyone, and he knew me more intimately than anyone, so if I was of no value to *him*, I was of no value at all. I was ashamed of myself not because I felt I had done anything wrong – that at least I could have put right. It was worse than that. I was ashamed of *myself*. I had been scrutinised thoroughly by the person who knew me best and found wanting in nearly every respect. This is a very deep pain.

Self-image

My self-image was at an all-time low. I looked in the mirror and saw old, lined, grey and fat. I suppose that's what happens when your husband exchanges you for a young, smooth, blonde, slimmer model. It can't be any easier though if you have been rejected in favour of an older woman, or a man, as some of my friends have been. And what if there *is* no one else, or no one that they are going to admit to? The message then from the one who knows you best is simply that they would prefer to be alone rather than look at you. Whatever form it comes in, the physical rejection penetrates deep into your psyche and that's when your self-image plummets to an all-time mega low. No wonder people fall into the arms of the first person who takes an interest! You feel that no one will ever take an interest again and who can blame them? I could not imagine that any man would ever find me attractive again. Old, lined, grey and fat. People who know me laugh at that. One friend used to say in desperation, "Just look in the mirror! You're young, slim and attractive!" But I couldn't see it. I tried, I really did, but I couldn't see it. It was like having one of those distorting mirrors from the fair in my bedroom – what I was seeing in the mirror was not an accurate picture.

What's in a name? (Part I)

The core of who I was in every way was rejected when my husband left. That left me with a crisis of identity. Who was I? What was valid or valuable about me? This crisis of identity meant that sometimes even the simplest of questions threw me completely. Take for example, "What's your name?" It seems such a simple question, doesn't it? I'm still not sure I can answer it. It's the first thing any stranger asks, and all of a sudden I didn't know how to answer it. I once hesitated over the question for so long that one kind lady inquired, "Do you speak English?" Even with such a basic question as "What's your name?" I had trouble. Who *was* I? It is more of an issue for women than for men in Western society, because women take their husband's name. I'd always been Mrs Jenny Clotworthy. (Well, I hadn't actually, but for reasons of privacy I'm not going to tell you my ex-husband's name, and Clotworthy seems a more interesting hypothetical name than Smith. I know a whole family of Clotworthys here in Devon, and very fine people they are too!) All my qualifications were in the name of Mrs Clotworthy and so were all my contracts, business papers, credit cards and bank accounts. Everything was in the Clotworthy name, *his name*. Yet I wasn't his any more, and I didn't want his name. I kept it for convenience and I kept it for the sake of connection with the children. It's not the name on the cover of this book. So there I am: I'm named Clotworthy but I'm not Clotworthy any more. So who am I? I could have reverted to my maiden name, but that didn't seem to fit either. I left my parental home over 20 years ago. I wasn't that person any more either.

Then there's the "Mrs". All my adult life I'd been "Mrs". It was a signal to the world. I belonged to someone; I wasn't available, and I'd got someone to love me. *Mr* Clotworthy, Smith, Brown or Blackadder is born with that name, grows with it and dies with it, whether single, married or divorced. His identity remains constant. A man's title tells you nothing of his marital status: a woman's does. "Mrs" no longer applied but I was hardly a "Miss" any more. It conjured up pictures of pigtails and pinafores! "Ms" is a good compromise. At least, it would be if every adult woman used it. Some business computers automatically generate it if you tick the "divorced or separated" box. I've never asked for the title "Ms" but it has been applied to me once it is known that I am divorced. It may be different in your part of the world, but for me "Ms" just signalled THIS WOMAN IS DIVORCED, which was not the first thing I necessarily wanted people to know about me. Oh dear. "Mrs Clotworthy" – it had been me for so long. Now I was no longer a member of the Clotworthy family. What's more, I was missing being "Mrs", with all it signified – that I was loved, respectable and secure. Even my name seemed to imply shame. "Miss" would raise questions about the children – did she have them out of wedlock? Ms implied hard-nosed feminist, which I wasn't, or divorcée, and why should they know? So I kept my name. I'm still known here as "Mrs Clotworthy" but I know it's no longer me. It makes me feel like a fraud. Like wearing a suit that isn't mine. Do separated men have the same problem? I suppose there is no change of name to highlight it but there are still the underlying problems of a change of identity.

So that left me with "Jenny". That was still me, wasn't it? Hmmm. Romeo and Juliet, Bonnie and Clyde, David and Jenny. The names had always gone together. (No, he's not called David either, but it's a good enough name.) It was tough signing Christmas cards just "Jenny". I kept putting the "Davidand". For so long it had been David and Jenny. "We are pleased to invite DavidandJenny to..." Maybe that's why I stopped getting invitations to things. Maybe no one knew whom they were inviting when they invited just "Jenny" without the "Davidand". Now the single word "Jenny" that I put on the end of letters and cards just reinforced the dreadful feeling that I was alone.

Back to basics, back to God

The only way I survived this sense of rejection, worthlessness and shame was to go back to basics and back to God. Actually, I don't think I even dared go back to God, because if I did I risked his rejection too, and whereas a man's rejection had devastated me, *God's* would have destroyed me. It was too big a risk to take, but God knew that. He drew me to himself. He continually told me throughout the first year, "I will never leave you nor forsake you." It became almost an in-joke. Everywhere I went I met that verse. I didn't know there were so many variations of that idea in the Bible. I must have tripped over all of them in that first year, and it wasn't because I was spending hours studying the Bible – I was too grief-stricken for that.

I suppose that was the foundation of my new life. I often said in those early days, "I've lost my husband but I haven't lost my God." Even when it didn't feel like it, I knew he was still there, probably because he kept making it plain. God is an independent being. He acts independently of me or my beliefs or mindset. I say that because it is fashionable at the moment to support people's faith. Faith is seen as A Good Thing. Psychologists know that people with a faith are more likely to make a good recovery. You are encouraged to keep your faith perspective, whatever it is. It is treated like something that belongs to you. *Your* personality, *your* upbringing, *your* faith all help you come to terms with the psychological blow.

I'm not so sure. I don't think my faith helped me at all. I think it went flying out of the window along with everything else when my world and my very self fragmented. Faith is just another word for trust, and my ability to trust had been dealt a deathblow. I couldn't trust anything. I didn't know what to trust; I didn't know any more what *was* trustworthy and what wasn't and I no longer had the means to discern it. I'd been maimed in the trust area. Friends would say, "He'll soon be back," or "You're better off without him," and they looked like cartoons mouthing something in Martian. What did it mean? How did they know? What could I trust? How did I begin to tell what I could trust?

In the same way I went to church and it looked like a play being acted. The characters looked overly happy. Surely they were acting. "God loves you," they say. "Right!"

you think, "God loves me. What does that mean? How do they know? What can I trust? How do I begin to trust a God who has just allowed me to experience an unbearable pain? Funny sort of love. Remind me, what was 'love' again?"

No, I don't think my faith helped. My trust in everything was gone. I *know* my religion was not a comfort to me. It didn't seem real. However, God is more than my faith and God is different from religion. God is not a construct of my mind or psyche. God is real. God *is*. God acts independently. God does not need our belief to exist. When all else has gone, God still is. In the depths of the night. In the silence of your room. In the innermost part of your very self. With nothing between you and the ends of the universe. God is. God is there. The force that holds the fragments together.

Healing of identity

I started by saying that I arrived at that Christian conference in a totally fragmented state. It was the best place I could have been. That whole site was saturated in prayer. Immediately God started the healing process in me. Looking back, it was as if he had choreographed the whole week for me, surrounding me with a sort of force field. "You are my Shield," said the Psalmist. He walked me through a personal timetable for that whole week. He placed me in a guest house nearby with one other guest. She was a quiet, confident, single Frenchwoman. It wasn't until halfway through the week that I found out that her husband had left her five years before. She was my visual aid. "God will take care of everything," she said. "Everything."

On site there was amazing worship, powerful teaching and a large, well-trained team of people who would pray with you. I didn't tell them what I wanted prayer for. They didn't ask me. They just asked God. That was very important to me. I was too fragile for anyone's good ideas. I was much too fragile for even the smallest platitude. I only wanted to know what God was saying.

Strangers prayed for me at least three times a day: just what the doctor ordered! They were safe because they were strangers. Even then I was frightened, praying desperately for the right people to approach for prayer, conscious that one wrong word could destroy me. God answered my prayers. He specifically chose people who would handle me with care. People who themselves had been broken or people who only listened to him, saying nothing from themselves. God covered many issues in that week. He set the foundations in many areas. He told me the stark and painful truth that nothing would ever be the same again, and gave me hope.

The first thing that God rebuilt into my shattered psyche was this fact. God is. His name is Jehovah Shammah – God who is there. This is what all else is built on. I was surprised to find myself appreciating, probably for the first time, God as Creator. He created everything. He created me. I am defined in terms of God. My mother and father may have been responsible for shaping me but in a very real sense I was conceived in the mind of God. I am his idea. Those characteristics I have were his idea. The whole of Psalm 139 is worth looking at, but in verses 13–18 we read: "You made all the delicate, inner parts of my body and knit me together in my mother's womb. Thank you for making me so wonderfully complex! Your workmanship is marvellous – and how well I know it. You watched me as I was being formed in utter seclusion, as I was woven together in the dark of the womb. You saw me before I was born. Every day of my life was recorded in your book. Every moment was laid out before a single day had passed. How precious are your thoughts about me, O God! They are innumerable! I can't even count them; they outnumber the grains of sand! And when I wake up in the morning, you are still with me!"

One lady, praying about fear of the future, said something that has always stayed in my mind. "Jesus IS your future." It was at the same time bitter and sweet. Another time, someone was praying for me and she said, "What do you see?" I didn't "see" anything but in my imagination there was a picture of a young dad tossing his little girl up into the air and catching her, saying "Mine!" with such pride and delight on his face. This then was where my identity was rooted. It was rooted in the basic and fundamental truth that I was God's. God constantly returns to this theme in restoring my sense of identity.

Healing on the inside

Dying to self and being recreated in his image is not a new idea. It is what is required of every Christian. The technical term for it is "sanctification". It is the process of becoming more like Jesus, which every Christian is engaged in. It's just that at the moment we are aware of the necessity of that process in our lives, in our very selves, because so much of the old has died and because so much deep stuff has been stirred up. A trauma like losing a loved one throws up deeper, underlying issues as well; fears and worries and insecurities and habits and patterns of thinking that have their roots in our childhood or in past blows and disappointments. Things like "Of course he left me – my parents never really wanted me; no one ever really wants me." My experience is that God allows these things to surface so that we can see them. It is painful to have them stirred up and brought into view, but my experience is that he allows this because he wants to deal with that issue in us.

Much has been written on inner healing and it is not

my place to go into it here. However, my experience is that God does heal on the inside. Forgiveness is a big key, of course, but God has lots of ways of healing our psyche. I've found skilled counselling very helpful, I think because it brings an objective view into the chaos of thoughts and emotions and helps you to see what is going on. Professional counsellors never tell you what to do; they listen and reflect back to you what you have said so that you can see what you are really thinking. Talking about it by itself is sometimes enough to solve a problem. Some things, once seen and acknowledged, lose their power.

Prayer has been essential in my healing. Sometimes talking about an issue has not been the solution, but has just identified the problem. In these cases other people's prayers have somehow cut to the root of the issue and removed it. Sometimes God tells other people what to pray for me. Prayer by itself has released me from various attitudes or past pains. "The prayer of a righteous man is powerful and effective" (James 5:16, NIV).

Tears are healing. Times and places where we can be free to cry are precious. A young friend of mine recently said, "When I first knew you four years ago you were crying just about every time I saw you!" He was right. He used to see me in church, and for me that was a safe place. I cried out all my tears and gave them to God. He thinks they are precious, you know. He collects them (Psalm 56:8). Never be ashamed of your tears. God told me that he accepted each one as a prayer, and as prayer was often an impossibility to me, and crying came very easily, that was a very reassuring thing to know.

Good-quality silence is healing. There are times and places where somehow it is easier to feel the peace or the presence of God. If you are lucky enough to have such a place, value it. Go there. I don't know how just being with God makes things better, but it does.

Understanding God's view of us in the Bible is

healing. God gave the most precious thing he had to buy us. We are children of God. Members of the ultimate Royal Family. We were created to a unique design. We are joint heirs with Christ. It's worth taking some of these ideas from time to time and really thinking about them, chewing them over until they sink in. God is always thinking about us individually as well. The Psalmist says, "How precious are your thoughts about me, O God! They are innumerable! I can't even count them; they outnumber the grains of sand! And when I wake up in the morning, you are still with me!" (Psalm 139:17–18).

Healing of self-image

The healing of your physical self-image is a difficult thing. You see, people can tell you that you look nice, but you just don't believe them. God kept sending me people to tell me I looked attractive, but I just didn't get it. In the end I decided to practise accepting the compliment even though I didn't understand it. I trained myself to smile and say "Thank you!" in a positive manner every time someone said something nice to me. This is, after all, only polite, and, by accepting the compliments when they were given, gradually the truth of what people were saying began to sink into my subconscious.

But the real advance in this area came when I was visiting Kenya. I was working with a team in a slum area where white people were rarely seen. We became fascinating exhibits as we walked through the slums in the company of the pastor and his wife (who were a normal black colour). People openly stared. Some of the children thought we were ghosts and ran away crying. Wherever we went, we were accompanied by cries of *"Msungu! Msungu!"* "White people! White people!" I have a photograph of one very brave little girl of about six who stared at me in serious and frank amazement. Surely human beings didn't come in that colour! What *was* I? (I had an instance of that feeling when I returned to England. Suddenly the whole population seemed to have contracted anaemia. They all looked like bloodless corpses walking around.)

I can only surmise that it was this unfamiliarity with the look of white people that caused the confusion over my age. I was staying for a month with a Kenyan family, and got to know them well. We were talking one day about our families. "How old is your first-born?" they asked. "He's 20," I replied. Consternation ensued. There was much counting on fingers and checking of English words. Were they really so shocked to find out I was so old? But, far from thinking me old, they thought I was a girl! They could not comprehend the fact that I had a 20-year-old son. What miracle was this? Surely I couldn't have become a mother at *five*?! Had the West discovered the secret of eternal youth? No? Then the only answer must be that God was blessing me greatly, because from the evidence of their own eyes, my beautiful hair (obviously yet another variation of msungu-blonde), my lovely skin, girl-like figure, and the way I danced, laughed and played with the children, I couldn't possibly be a day over 25 – well, say 26 to 30, but that was really pushing it! I laughed and laughed, and in vain tried to tell them that my hair was grey, but they were truly perplexed. I think God was trying to tell me something...

Healing of rejection

Finally, don't forget that our God is a living God. He acts in our lives to help and heal in very individual ways. He deals with each one of us as a unique individual. He does it his way.

Here's one example. I had just come off the phone and I was distraught. I had been trying to make some moves towards reconciliation with my estranged husband but I'd got nowhere. What hit me as I put the phone down was that the coldness and distance of our conversation had been expressed in the tones of a voice at once so familiar and beautiful to me. The contrast was too great. It hit the core of my pain and I sat on the floor incapacitated with grief, unable to move, unable to do anything but cry. There are moments you just can't cope with. This was one of them. I didn't know what to do with the pain. I tried to pray. There is only one prayer in that sort of situation, the unspoken cry of "help". It didn't help. I couldn't get control of myself.

I reached for the ever-present hankie to blow my nose and as I did so I blinked my eyes open. What I saw through the mist of tears, I didn't believe. Across the room directly in front of me I saw projected onto the plain white door of my kitchen a shadow picture of a crucified man. I blinked the tears away, convinced that the image would disappear with the tears, like a mirage. It didn't; it just became clearer. I could see it as real as the day and holding steady. Like some piece of modern art painted in bold clear strokes of grey, I could see the torso and arms, the straight beams of the cross behind, the head bowed so gently, so meekly, and the suggestion of a crown of thorns – all painted in shadow on the door.

Now I was worried – this was weird! My sobs began to subside as my mind went into overdrive. Was it a vision? I stared at it, expecting it to disappear as mysteriously as it had come. I closed my eyes deliberately and opened them again. It was still there, still broadcasting its mute message of empathy and understanding. For a good ten minutes I must have stared at it. It remained, unmoving. Finally, I was intrigued. "How have you done that?" I said, and lifted my heavy heart and swollen face and slowly walked across the room to look at it and touch it. Shadows. They must be coming from somewhere. I lifted my hand until it too made a shadow on the door, and traced it back to its source.

Suddenly the mystery was revealed. Suspended from the ceiling over the Aga was a drying rack from which an assortment of clothes were hanging, some draped, some on hangers. One of the boys' sweatshirts, drying on a hanger, had somehow twisted round and got itself wedged at an angle behind another, empty, hanger and the whole thing was caught in the beam of one of the ceiling spotlights that illuminated our kitchen. The result was a beautiful, gracious, life-sized shadow-image projected onto the back of the kitchen door.

I was amazed. The drying washing had never caused such an effect before, and it never has since. I am still amazed by it. I showed the boys the effect when they came bursting into the kitchen looking for their tea. "Oh, yeah," they said matter-of-factly. "When's dinner?" To them it meant nothing, but to me it was a beautiful creative act that got me through an awful moment. It was a message of profound empathy and care, and a means of transforming what could have been yet another traumatic memory into a beautiful recollection of God's amazing timing, tenderness and love.

The healing process takes time and, as you can see, God used and is using many and varied ways to restore me. Sometimes it was the genuine comment of a friend, "You look nice today!" Sometimes an intervention that I couldn't explain away, like the one I've just related. Sometimes it was an insight gained from Scripture that helped. I happened to be reading Matthew's account of the crucifixion where the people are mocking Jesus calling him to come down from the cross. In the version I was reading the leaders of the community follow it up with, "Yes! Let God rescue him – if he WANTS him" (Matthew 27:43). It was that "If he wants him" that broke my heart. It made me cry and I didn't know why. However,

I did recognise God in that. I find that if I have a big reaction to a small thing it is because there is an underlying issue to be sorted out or healed. God is drawing my attention to it. Here I was empathising so much with the idea that Jesus might be unwanted because I knew what that felt like: *I* felt so unwanted. The healing, of course, was in the same verse. Jesus knew what it was to be perfectly loving and yet be totally unwanted. He understood rejection from the inside. Yet in his rejection he was making us all acceptable to God. Physically and emotionally, he was made to feel shame on the cross. He understands shame. Maybe that is what Paul means when he says, "He was made sin for us". He became all that was filthy and disgusting and shameful. Yet he had nothing to be ashamed about. Knowing that he has experienced this so much more than I have and understands what it is like so much more than I do is somehow healing in itself.

What's in a name? (Part II)

God is in the business of changing names. The Bible records lots of times when people had their names changed to show they were now different inside. Jacob the deceiver became Israel, man of God. Abram (exalted father) became Abraham (father of a multitude). On God's promise Sarai became Sarah, princess, with the promise that she would have a child and there would be kings amongst her descendents (Genesis 17 if you'd like to read about it). In a song by D. J. Butler the change of name shows a change of identity:

"I will change your name, you shall no longer be called, wounded, outcast, lonely or afraid. I will change your name, your new name shall be confidence, joyfulness, overcoming one, faithfulness, friend of God, one who seeks my face."*

Notice there are more positives than negatives. That's

so God. He gives back more than was taken. I recorded that in my diary on 1st September 1998. At the time it was a promise for the future. Well, we're in a new millennium now and I've got a new self-image. I've got a new, very positive identity. Can you tell? It was a long journey, but I got there.

Chapter 8

What About Sex?

If you are currently in a satisfying sexual relationship you do not need this chapter. Please skip it and turn to the next one, which is really interesting. Thank you.

(That space was for all the happily married and sexually-fulfilled counsellors, and interested friends, to leave.)

Right! Now that we are alone, all together now... after three... one, two, THREE...

AAAAARRRRRRRGGGGGGGHHHHHHH!!!!!!!!!

That's better! But not a lot. The problem is that there is no substitute for sex. Chocolate is quite good (you probably won't understand that unless you are female), but if you have known a good sex life nothing else makes up for the loss.

In the early days, dealing with my own sexuality was not a problem. Loss of a sex life was a loss I felt intensely, but it was just one of the huge losses I was experiencing. In a sense it was insignificant for me compared to the loss of the love and companionship and daily presence of my husband. The loss of my children and family life was even more intense, and dealing with the grief and readjustment of the whole process took up all my energy, and more. Oh yes, I had those "I'll show him!" feelings, where for a mad and angry moment I considered getting dressed up and going out on the pull. "If he can, why can't I?" But actually, pride stopped me. After all, why should I descend to their level?

Then there was the vague idea that God wouldn't like it, but if I'm being honest, the true reason was probably that my self-image and confidence were at such a low ebb I could never have seen it through. Those of us who have known sex within a loving marriage don't really want to settle for less. I couldn't imagine anyway that anyone would want me again. I couldn't imagine that I would ever be able to love again or to become *that* intimate with anyone again. So at that time I was angry at having to accept such a permanent loss but I was really too busy dealing with my grief for it to be a major problem. For me the trouble came later, when I was over the initial grief and gaining confidence and beginning to go out and about again...

Propositioned!

I got ready for the party and decided I looked good, and wondered who might be there. By now I was really looking for some physical comfort, and I wondered what I (with a few drinks inside me) might do if somebody offered. Yes, I really thought that.

When I arrived, somebody commented, "What an entrance!" and I felt a little embarrassed. It was a fancy-dress party and I'd gone, with wings and antennae, in full fairy rig. The problem was, no one else had bothered dressing up. The embarrassment knocked any siren thoughts out of my head. Anyway everyone was in couples or much older than me. So I concentrated on getting a glass of wine down me and demolishing the garlic bread. A male friend, let's call him Mike, whispered some very kind words about my appearance on a couple of occasions, but I thought he'd just noticed my discomfiture and was being encouraging. However, after we had eaten we got into conversation, and he repeated his compliments, which I accepted graciously. He began to make certain suggestions, which I jokingly laughed off as very kind compliments!

He pursued the matter. This was new ground for me. Having married young I had never been propositioned before and wasn't quite sure what to do about it. So I turned the conversation to the serious discussion of how easy it was to have men friends when you were married (with the emphasis on FRIEND) and how I wasn't quite sure how to deal with it now I was single again. So he offered to give me some practice.

"Seriously," he said, looking me in the eye, "I don't beat around the bush, I come right out and say what I mean... I don't know what's happened to you but you're looking VERY good and I do find you very attractive. All you've got to do is phone up and invite me round for a cup of coffee and I'll know what you mean... "

He wasn't drunk; he wasn't lecherous. He spoke friend to friend, very genuine and very straight. It wasn't a joke; it was a genuine offer. Thank goodness I didn't fancy him!

Reactions

Immediately I felt surprised. When I realised that he was being serious, very honest, and it wasn't a joke, I felt very good and very flattered. I then felt extremely powerful, boosted by the idea that I could "get a man" if I wanted to. That was a new feeling! Then I felt guilty – was it my fault, for being dressed in a sensual way? Mind you, a dress that goes from neck to ankle is hardly provocative. Maybe it was the wings that turned him on.

When I got back home I began to feel vulnerable. I

didn't want to be pursued! He knew where I lived! I made sure the doors and windows were locked.

Then I began to be suspicious of the other male friends and acquaintances I had. Is that why Wayne was coming round and is that what Fred really meant? (I am making up these names, but you get the idea.) Was there more to this "Can I drop by for a cup of coffee?" than met the eye? Was it a code everyone used?

Then I began to feel very sorry for, and disappointed in, Mike. Was he really that shallow? Was that as far as his understanding of sex went? Let's have a good time for an hour or two, no harm done as long as it's mutually understood?

Then I felt rather used, unclean. What right had he to look at me that way? I thought he was a friend!

Finally I was left feeling angry. What right had he got to think he could do me a favour and then just walk off again as if nothing had happened! What about deceiving his wife? Did he think she wouldn't mind? Did he think I would do that to her?

As you can see, I was in a state of confusion. It was not an issue I'd had to deal with in the previous 25 years! It certainly is an issue that arises as soon as you get some confidence back in yourself. At this stage, though, I was fortunate in that I was only dealing with the idea, not with my own sexuality. I hadn't thought I'd ever have the opportunity again. It slowly dawned on me that I was single again and that in our culture single people are seen as available for a sexual relationship. I obviously had some thinking to do.

It took me by surprise, as up to that point I hadn't even thought of myself as being attractive to anyone else. On the other hand I *had* gone out thinking, "If anyone offers tonight I'll be straight into bed with them, and who cares!", only to find that someone did offer, and I wasn't straight into bed with them because *I* cared. I *did* have principles and values and standards. We all have an unspoken line that we are not prepared to cross. I found out that I didn't even consider taking him up on his kind offer because I wasn't prepared to hurt his wife. Or was it simply the principle that I wasn't prepared to have sex with someone I didn't fancy? I hope I'm not being too frank for you here. It's just that I found I had to reconsider my principles all over again from the very basics.

There are people out there ready to give you what they think you are missing. There are others happy to take from you what *they* are missing. In the middle of it all there is you, missing it. It helps to do some thinking about this before the situation arises.

The real problems came later, when my confidence began to return and I got to know and like myself and realise slowly that I was an attractive person. This was a long process of healing and readjustment, which to some extent is still going on. My encounter with "Mike" was positive in the end, as it began to convince me that I was still sexually attractive. An idea I hadn't considered before. I hadn't had to think about it since I was a teenager.

What happened next showed me that I wasn't a teenager any more. It also taught me that the world has changed in its attitude to sex since I was a teenager.

Casual sexual relationships

"You want to go out and enjoy yourself," said the husband of a good friend of mine. "Just go out and find a man and have a good time, nothing serious, no strings attached." He meant it sincerely. He was talking about casual sexual relationships. It is a solution that many divorced people employ. It showed me how society has changed since I was a teenager. It's no longer thought of as a shameful thing to have sex before marriage. Indeed, it's almost expected.

I'm not convinced though that it is possible to have a sexual relationship "with no strings attached". I think there are always strings attached – emotional and spiritual bonds which are hard to break. We even talk in English about "emotional entanglements". I had enough problems to deal with; I didn't need any more emotional entanglements to add to them. I'd seen the pain of enough rebound relationships to know I didn't want that. Also, as I've already said, those of us who have known a good sexual relationship in marriage don't want to settle for less. After all, as *The Message* puts it at the end of 1 Corinthians 6:

> There's more to sex than mere skin on skin. Sex is as much spiritual mystery as physical fact. As written in Scripture, "The two become one". Since we want to become spiritually one with the Master, we must not pursue the kind of sex that avoids commitment and intimacy, leaving us more lonely than ever—the kind of sex that can never "become one". There is a sense in which sexual sins are different from all others. In sexual sin we violate the sacredness of our own bodies, these bodies that were made for God-given and God-modeled love, for "becoming one" with another. Or didn't you realize that your body is a sacred place, the place of the Holy Spirit? Don't you see that you can't live however you please, squandering what God paid such a high price for? The physical part of you is not some piece of property belonging to the spiritual part of you. God owns the whole works. So let people see God in and through your body.

Mind you, knowing what you should and shouldn't do is different from actually doing it.

Yes, I knew that casual sexual relationships were a

no-no for me as a committed Christian, so how did I find myself nearly doing just that?

It took me by surprise too. I knew him quite well. He was friendly and pleasant, and I used to see him from time to time around the town. We got on well, talking about everything. I appreciated his company and he appreciated mine. It is nice to be appreciated. He invited me back for coffee a few times. Just coffee. We became friends. Because of the age difference between us I saw no romantic involvement arising. Just to make sure that we understood the situation, we used to talk about that a lot, valuing our friendship for what it was and no more. I really liked having some male company again and I really liked the fact that someone was enjoying my company. We laughed a lot and talked deeply. Life was a lot less lonely.

One day he asked if he could kiss me. I näively expected a fatherly, affectionate kiss on the cheek. What I got was a passionate kiss on the lips. What happened next surprised me. I liked it! I *really* liked it! That's when I discovered I wasn't a teenager any more. When I was a teenager I went out with several boys. The pattern of our relationships was more or less the same. You held hands and kissed on the lips for a few weeks (that's what "going out" meant really, as opposed to being "just friends"), and then the kissing got more passionate and extended. That led on to greater explorations. My friends and I had a star system to indicate how far we'd got (it's confession time here now, folks!). I know the boys had various systems and various codes too – you know the type of thing: above the waist, below the waist, over clothes, under clothes – it could take six months to get up to *three* stars! But that was back then. I'm talking about now. He kissed me, and my body liked it. You never forget how to swim. It'd been a long time since I'd been swimming, but once I'd jumped in I was right there and striking out for the deep end!

Let's just say that it took approximately ten minutes to get to the five-star stage. The ONLY reason why I didn't end up sleeping with him that day is that he was a total gentleman, and knowing my religious views he stopped and didn't take me to bed. I would have gone with him.

Are you shocked? I was. I was shocked at myself. I was shocked at the strength of my feelings. I think I learnt for the first time exactly how strong the sex drive is. You see, I *knew* that there was no future in this relationship. We got on well as friends but he wasn't a potential husband. What's more, although there was an ease of communication and a chemistry between us, I wasn't actually attracted to him physically. Nevertheless, once we kissed I was gone!

It was the speed of it all that surprised me. Logic and principles went out of the window and my body took over. If you are really shocked, PLEASE go and read the next chapter. However, if this is all sounding very familiar, stay and explore it with me. I know I'm not the only one to have had experiences like this. A lady I met on a train once confessed to me that she had found herself in bed with the *window cleaner*. Afterwards she couldn't for the life of her think why!

Thinking about it

Looking back, I decided that it hadn't all been quite as sudden as I'd thought. There were patterns of thinking and behaviour that had led that far. To save us all embarrassment, I am going to talk about cream cakes.

If you are on a diet it may be hard to resist cream cakes. One day you go to the shop, buy one and eat it. Then you wonder how it happened! Well, the truth is you weren't just propelled to the shop by some irresistible force that day to buy cream cakes. A lot of things had happened before that. First, you were eating your low-fat Weight Watchers biscuits with slight boredom and you began to reminisce about cream cakes. Your mind compared the two and there was no doubt – cream cakes definitely had something over the "it's-so-good-for-you" range of specialised low-fat food now in your larder.

As the days pass, you reminisce more and more. After all, there's nothing wrong with thinking about it, is there? You remember all the different variations of cake. Cream doughnuts, chocolate éclairs... Which was better? You can hardly remember, but you think it was those cream-filled apple pastries...

One day you are flicking through a magazine and there is a full-colour spread of real cream cakes. They shouldn't be allowed to do it! But they do, and you have a good look. It's an advert for the new patisserie counter at the hypermarket that's opening outside town. Their cream doughnuts look rather factory-made, though, and not half as appetising as the ones they used to sell in that little shop in town. Just to make sure, next time you're in town, you walk past that shop and look in the window. After all, there is no harm in looking, is there?

You were right! Their cream cakes are a much better quality! In fact, the shop is so good that you begin to go in there to buy your bread. You are allowed to eat *bread* and you know that you won't be buying any cream cakes. You can walk past the cream cakes with no trouble. Just having a look from time to time. You often compliment the shopkeeper on the quality of her cream cakes. After all, you may not be able to eat them, but you know that many people do, and they *are* veritable works of art.

One day you buy one along with your bread. It's eating it that is the problem, you reason; *buying* it is not wrong. You just put it in the fridge to look at. It's there every time you go to the fridge and you are not tempted to eat it once! By the end of the day, you know you are going to have to throw it away, but as you pick it up to dispose of it you reason to yourself that a quick lick of cream is not the same as actually eating it. There's no one around and surely there's no harm in just having a lick of it? You decide you can go that far, as long as you don't actually eat it. So you take a lick of cream. Ten seconds later you find, to your utmost surprise, that you have disposed of the cream cake in a way you hadn't anticipated. "I just don't know how it happened!" you confess to Weight Watchers at the next meeting!

You know what I mean. It doesn't help us to think about, look at or read about things we can't have. At the moment I'm not watching much television, buying even mainstream magazines or reading those cheap romantic novels. I find it makes my life a lot easier. People who are in satisfying sexual relationships will not understand this. They may think you a little prudish. They don't see the subliminal messages in much of the modern media. I never used to. I do now, and I find it helps me to avoid it as much as possible. In the words of *The Message* from Philippians 4: "Summing it all up, friends, I'd say you'll do best by filling your minds and meditating on things true, noble, reputable, authentic, compelling, gracious—the best, not the worst; the beautiful, not the ugly; things to praise, not things to curse." There is a connection between what we think about and what we do. Talking about what we think about and what we do...

Masturbation

The next solution offered by some is masturbation (Shock! Horror! She used the word!), which can ease the tension but, as anyone who has tried it knows, is a temporary solution to a physical problem. There is no prohibition against it in the Bible. The problem with Onan (Genesis 38:8–10) is not that he was doing it but that he was refusing his brother's widow her rights under the law at the time (Deuteronomy 25:5–6). If there is nothing specifically written against the actual act, then whether it is right or wrong depends on what your motivation is and what is going on in the mind. Masturbation can provide considerable relief of sexual tension, but if it is just bolstering a dubious thought-life then it may simply serve to increase the frustration in the long run. (Phew! Aren't you glad that all the others are safely reading the next chapter!)

Sublimation

One way of dealing with all that excess sexual energy is not to repress it but to channel it into something else. I found that exercise helps. It's not an answer as such, but it helps. It also has added side-effects. It keeps you fit and healthy. It counteracts depression. It can be a great outlet for anger and it helps you sleep. Walking, jogging, swimming, cycling, line dancing, aerobics, squash, tennis, keep-fit tapes – whatever fits in with your lifestyle and whatever you enjoy. It helps. A bit.

If you have the time and energy you may be able to start that project you always wanted to do. Learn an instrument, get those extra qualifications, help out at the women's refuge or the old people's home, go trekking in the Himalayas, take up photography, rediscover your artistic talents or write a book! Decorate your home, redesign the garden, take up a new form of spirituality. The key is to find something you really want to do and then lose yourself in it. When you really enjoy something it doesn't feel like an effort and there is a great sense of achievement afterwards. I probably shouldn't say this, but there's an added sense of achievement if it is something your ex couldn't do or wouldn't let you do.

There *are* other thrills in life

Why is it that you always want what you can't have at the moment? Sometimes in this sex thing you just have to get it in proportion. I'm reminded of a study I read about years ago. Psychologists noted that when a group of navy personnel were on a long tour of duty without shore leave or visits home to their families the insides of their locker doors were covered with photos of wives and girlfriends and beautiful ladies. Understandable enough. The interesting thing to me was that when the same personnel were sent on a tour of duty *with* shore leave and visits from loved ones, but were denied good food, things changed round! They were being fed on a boring diet of dried food, pills and emergency rations and suddenly the girls came off the inside of their locker doors and were replaced with pictures of steaks, cream cakes and gourmet meals! You crave what you are missing and it can get out of proportion. Despite what almost every soap opera on television would have us believe, most people are not spending all their time thinking about or involved in some new sexual intimacy! The vast majority of life consists of other things. Here's a diary entry from just after Christmas last year:

Yesterday I really felt a lack of intimacy. The lack of a familiar person to share with. I called in at Melanie's and she soon put me straight. "Its all in the mind, Jen," she said. "It's what you make of it – you can choose *what you think." Her wise advice was to acknowledge the thoughts, then put them to one side. Choose to think differently. That woman* knows *how to do single! She told me of the early-morning run she'd been on, frosty grass, morning colours around the headland, the sea, the creek, the sun rising in beautiful shades of soft orange and red. "We think we need*

partners but that's more than any man could give you!"
she said.

I wasn't convinced, but I got to thinking about it. After
all, much sex is run-of-the-mill, samey, boring even. And
there are other thrills. As I walked back, I thought of some
of them. The breathtaking view from the top of the Long
Mynd in Shropshire, or the deer in Lake Nakuru game
park, Kenya, exquisitely beautiful and staring full at us.
The ecstasy of worship that puts you on a different plane.
The deep unspoken joy of being able to share heart-to-heart
with a friend. The incredible fulfilment of teaching in the
slums of Nairobi. The beautiful intimacy of God drawing
close in a silent room. The softness and loving trust of a
little child who cuddles close and falls asleep in your arms.
The excitement of a chance meeting that turns out to have
huge significance. The satisfaction in being able to spend
hours uninterrupted on a creative task. Learning new
skills, taking on more responsibility at work and getting
the credit for it. There are other thrills and there are other
fulfilments. I'm not saying they make up for lack of inti-
macy exactly, but they are pluses in this life that I may not
otherwise have had. And it helps to keep things in propor-
tion. Sex is not the be-all-and-end-all of life. It is one expe-
rience amongst many.

Intimacy and sexuality

There are two sides to sex, or two things we gain out of it
(besides the gift of children). It meets our physical need
to be touched and our psychological need to be intimate.
Casual sex might meet our need to be physically touched,
but without commitment and a real knowing of the other
person our need for intimacy and love is not met, and
that is why our sense of pain and rejection gets worse.
However, on the other hand, it is possible to be in a close,
caring relationship without being sexual. In other words,

it is possible to have intimate relationships without having sexual relationships.

The Ancient Greeks knew this, as shown by their four different words for love. *Eros* is the Greek word for sexual love. *Philos* is the word for non-sexual love, love between parents and children, for example, or between close friends. *Storge* is that strong liking of something as in "I love pasta" and *agape* is the self-giving love sometimes shown by human beings for people they don't know well, like a firefighter giving their life ("greater love has no man...") to save a stranger.

The trouble with English is that we just have the one word to cover all types of love, and from the songs in the charts you'd think that all love was sexual love or eros. Eros is a beautiful thing, but so is philos, and it is possible to have friends so close that your friendship is a type of love. You have an intimacy, even though it is not a sexual intimacy. This is an intimacy of the soul or spirit. We talk about soul mates, don't we? I have been lucky enough to have some friends I can count as soul mates.

There is a type of intimacy with God that is available to us too. In Hebrew it is called *da'at elohim* – knowledge of God. It's the intimate knowing *of* God as opposed to knowing *about* God. Feelings come and go, sometimes with a storm-like intensity, but I have known the close presence of God, in both the joyful times and the grief-stricken times, and there is *nothing* like it.

What does the Bible say?

"It is quite true that the way to live a godly life is not an easy matter. But the answer lies in Christ who came to earth and, as a man, was proved spotless and pure in his spirit" (1 Timothy 3:16, Living Bible). Jesus did it. Jesus lives in us. Paul expected his young churches to be examples of godly and pure living. "Ah yes," I said, "but I bet they didn't have the same temptations and problems in the first century as we have in our libertine twenty-first century society!" I really believed that, until I began to look at the background to the church at Corinth. Few societies today are as libertine. Sexual relations were allowed with almost anyone. It was a normal part of life, institutionalised within the old Greek religion of the time. These new Corinthian Christians had grown up with the sexual values and practices of their Greek society, and they had to be taught that this was not behaviour that was pleasing to the God they were now committed to. Paul was asking a lot of them. But ask it he did.

I don't know why, but we tend to think of sexual sin as being worse than any other sin. In Galatians chapter five Paul lists the results of following our human nature (in some translations called "the flesh") rather than following our spiritual nature (what God-living-in-us wants). Sure enough, immorality, impurity and indecency are there, but so are jealousy, bad temper, divisions, party spirit (factions), selfishness, envy and drunkenness. So, if we did sleep with the window cleaner or visit that dodgy Internet site, and we are regretting it now and feeling guilty about it, don't think it's any harder for God to forgive *that* than our or other people's selfishness or bad temper. Sin is sin. And, thank goodness, forgiveness is forgiveness. God forgives and forgets everything you've done, if you just admit it to him and repent. But don't go and make a habit of it again – it's not good for you!

Look at what Jesus had to say about the woman caught in a sexual act with someone she wasn't married to (by the way, who exactly was *watching*? And where was the man?). He said to the men who were accusing her, "Whichever one of you has committed no sin can throw the first stone" (John 8:7). In other words, "Why do you think her sins are worse than yours?"

Jesus' treatment of the Samaritan woman at the well

is worth a close look (John 4). He looked at her and knew she had had many dubious marriages and sexual relationships, but he treated her as a theologian, debating issues of spirituality and ways of worship, not debating the rights and wrongs of her past. He was then happy to accept her as an evangelist to her people (verse 39). It's a stark contrast, isn't it, to the attitude of some religious leaders today?

Having said that, the New Testament is full of warnings against getting caught up in sexual immorality. When the first Jewish leaders of the Christian church had to decide which of the old Jewish laws the Gentile Christians should be required to keep, they came up with very few, but right there in the middle was KEEP YOURSELVES FROM SEXUAL IMMORALITY. It's all over Paul's letters. 1 Corinthians 5, Galatians 5, 1 Thessalonians 4... this teaching occurs throughout the New Testament. I must say I was surprised when I actually looked at the extent of it. But it's there and it's unequivocal. Sex is as God intended it when it is between a man and a woman who are married. If you have given your life to God and accepted the sacrifice of Jesus as your Saviour, receiving his Spirit into the core of your being, then the new life he has given you does not involve having sex with anyone unless they are your husband or wife. (Shall we all go back to the beginning of the chapter and scream again?) I may marry again – most divorced people do – but until then I have decided that, for me, being single means being celibate.

It's worth waiting for

There is no doubt that once that initial period of grief and lack of confidence is over, this is one of the most difficult areas for divorced people to deal with. After all, we are not teenagers any more, tentatively exploring the whole area of our sexuality. We do know what we are missing. Sometimes it all seems too difficult to live with, or rather to live *without*. At those times it is easy to forget that sex was God's idea and that he gives us guidelines for dealing with it, not to restrict us, but so that we can enjoy the very best.

God's ideal is that sex is the physical expression of a oneness on every level. Then it has depths of meaning and mutual satisfaction not available elsewhere. Some young friends of mine were surprised the other day to find "having sex" described as "lovemaking". It was to them an old-fashioned term they hadn't come across. They thought it was a beautiful phrase! To "make love" is to express a love that is already there. The deeper the love and trust between two people, the better the lovemaking. This is worth waiting for! As Paul points out, there is a deep mystery in the sexual act. It is not just the sharing of some nice sensations, it is the sharing of your very selves. That is why it can be used as a metaphor for the unity between Christ and the church. God sharing his very self with the church, who in response gives her all in abandonment to her God. It is a mystery, and as such it is almost impossible to describe. All our analysis of the biological and psychological effects of sex does not come close to describing the mystery of it. However, I caught a glimpse of the mystery at the recent wedding of two friends of mine.

They talked about the faith they shared and the dreams and visions they had for their life together in God. They talked about their meeting and how their friendship had grown and the fun they had in enjoying each other's company. They talked about the difficulties of trusting in a society where many relationships are temporary and about the seriousness with which they were taking this step, deliberately committing their whole lives to each other, giving the gift of themselves to each other for as long as they lived. And throughout it all the love and sincerity that they had between them was beautifully evident in the way they looked into each other's eyes. I can't describe it; it was SO beautiful. Unity of spirit and soul expressed in commitment and soon-to-be unity of body. That is true oneness. It was SUCH a precious thing that, watching it, I made myself a sort of inner vow. I said to God, "If there is the smallest chance that I might have a future relationship like *that*, I will wait. Even if it takes years, I will wait and not settle for second best." (*Second* best! What did I mean, second best? What I had thought about doing was two hundred and fifty-*fourth* best compared to what they had!) What I saw there between them was incredibly precious. God's best is certainly worth waiting for!

Chapter 9

Will I Ever Love Again?

Is love a myth?

Divorce had left me with the feeling that romantic love was somehow an illusion. Watching romantic movies certainly gave me that impression. Here is what I wrote in my diary one evening:

Love. Is it a myth? I've just enjoyed yet another romantic film about true love winning in the end. Is that all there is to write about in the movies today? Is that the only theme of books, films and soaps? Is it all that people long for? Love and the happy ending? I want to fall for it, but it's not reality. It's not real life. Oh here's another one. Cher is starring now. Her real-life love life was nothing to write home about! Anyone can have a film romance. The actor is paid to do it. It's not real. So why do we think it is? Why do we want to believe it is? I suppose it's better than films about people killing each other. It made me happy. I really wanted it to work out for them and of course it did. It wasn't reality. Happy endings are compulsory. They sell films.

Rejection makes you feel as if love is a myth. Betrayal makes you feel like a used and filthy floor cloth, repulsive to anyone that dares pick it up. Deceit leaves you believing nothing, trusting no one. Anger makes you want to hurt other people, to use them as you have been used. I couldn't imagine ever loving again. How could I ever take the risk of that pain again?

So it took me by surprise when it happened. I've already told you in chapter seven about how God went about restoring my self-image and self-esteem. After some of those foundations were established in my life, positive feelings for the opposite sex started to return and I had no idea at all how to cope with them. It was like being a teenager again.

Teenager feelings

I was so used to strange emotions hitting me from time to time that I thought at first it was just another variation of those, just a part of the process. I remember turning up to a prayer meeting in church to find a visitor there. He was a man I had met once or twice at bigger conferences. He was divorced, too; we'd talked about this. What was he doing here? I took one look at him and my heart started pounding in my ears and I lost control of my arms and legs. They started gesticulating wildly in time with my voice, which had suddenly become high-pitched. I beat a hasty retreat. What was going on? I was used to experiencing some strange emotions and reactions, but this was weird! I took refuge in a cup of tea.

"What's going on?" I asked God. I hated these unexplained emotions that hit me without warning.

"You like him," said God.

"No, I don't!" I replied. "I don't even know him!"

"You'd like to get to know him, though."

"No, I wouldn't – he's really not my type."

God held his peace. He's very good at inscrutable.

I returned to the meeting and greeted everyone warmly EXCEPT this one man, yet I was acutely aware of his every move. People were in a stage of transition, moving to other rooms, preparing to start the next session. It was as if I had antennae tuned in to his movements and constantly reporting back. I didn't understand it at all. Was he going to stay for the afternoon or leave? WHY was that important to me? Then he made up his mind, said goodbye to one or two people and headed for the door. For a moment he hesitated and looked back. My eyes caught him, framed in the doorway, blue jeans, white shirt, jacket slung over his shoulder. *Wow!* I knew *that* feeling! I bowed my head in defeat. "OK, God, you win. He *is* my type." I never thought I'd have feelings for a man again. Now I found I most definitely did. My next question was, "What on earth do I do now?"

Our paths crossed only once in a while, so I had plenty of time to try to analyse what was happening to me. Every so often we coincided in the same place, functioning quite well in a group but often overcome with embarrassment one to one. It was ages before we JUST about got to the point of NEARLY being able to hold a conversation with each other when we met! He was so, so nervous! So nervous! He reminded me of one of those beautiful African deer, the ones with the ultra-smooth lines, tan and white, with the go-faster black stripe down the middle. The stags stand and look at you with heads held high. "How can anything so beautiful be male?" you think, but male they most definitely are. They stare at you so regally, holding your gaze. Then, as soon as you make a noise or the slightest movement towards them, they twitch as if their whole body were one muscle, and are suddenly four feet off the ground and bounding away into the distance! Thompson's gazelles, I think.

I had the same sort of experience with this man. Once when I was trying to give him a message I saw the reaction clearly. His exact words were, "Hi there! (twitch) Sorry, I must just catch Nicky!" (bound, bound). I did manage to catch up with him again. I stalked gently through the bush (sorry, car park), and approached him obliquely while he was off guard, talking to his son. Finally I delivered the message I had for him. What a relief to see him smile. "Cool," he says, and then there's a pause and a string of words issues from him in a stream of panic, something so incoherent that I couldn't catch even the gist of it.

"Bleeeeuer gureluk urk eeer euuueeek!" he said, with a look of desperation on his face.

"Pardon?" I said, wondering if he was fluent in Martian. He looked away, raised his eyes to the sky, took a deep breath and carefully formed the words again, one by one.

"Are you…" cough… deep breath… "Are… you, back … at (gaining confidence now) schoolnextweek?"

"Yes," I replied. It took a millisecond to say.

I knew that wasn't helpful. The expression of blank amazement in his eyes told me it wasn't helpful. But it was all I could manage. It was difficult enough even to hear *that* over the deafening beating of my heart reverberating in my ears.

The boy looked at each of us, turning his face from one to the other. "Adults! Can you believe them?!" was written all over his face.

What is this nervousness that turns two articulate adults into teenagers? Unable to hold eye contact. Unable to hold a conversation. Words tumbling incoherently! Honestly! They really don't make sense! Stuttering streams of gibberish from which the odd phrase tumbles: "Hi there!" or "Cool!" What is it that affects the nervous system so? Flushing the face. Disabling co-ordination. Arms and legs can take on a life of their own, you know, dancing off or gesticulating wildly. Why? Why does it need such immense reserves of self-control just to stand still? Or to frame a simple question like, "Have you had a good holiday?" It was exactly like being a teenager! I can't tell you how confusing that was at my age. It was menopausal feelings I was expecting, not teenager ones! It was ludicrous!

The feelings didn't go away, though. Just the memory of his smile warmed my heart. The mention of his name made my heart beat faster. The sight of him softened me from the depths of my being out to the edges, depriving me of rational thought, taking away my power of speech. My prepared speeches flew out of my head, dissolving in the air, irreclaimable. Very strange symptoms. We skirted round each other like children. Blushing and incapable. This is two grown adults I'm talking about!

It threw me into a sort of desperation, a different sort of desperation from the one I was used to. It came out of positive feelings, not negative. I didn't know what to do! If I were fifteen I'd say, "I've got a crush on him." I'd get my best friend to tell him, "She fancies you!" If I were fifteen I'd have sent him a Valentine's Day card, big, bright red and crazy, with my address on the back!

That's the trouble, isn't it? I hadn't felt like this since I was fifteen. I didn't have the vocabulary any more. Or the techniques. I certainly didn't have the experience! But I did have baggage. We both had baggage. Once bitten, twice shy. Especially when the dog that bit was the pet dog, known and trusted for years. Before it went mad, that is. Best not to risk that again at all. We find ourselves with gaping emotional wounds and quick protective reactions. Fear! Fear of involvement. Fear of commitment. Fear of the future. Fear of failure. Fear of rejection. Gaps! Gaping holes where wife, husband, family, in-laws, home, sanity used to be. Worries! I'm too grey, too lined, too unfit, too damaged, too fat, too thin, too set in my ways, too OLD for this! This is young person's territory, isn't it? All that (and more) is mixed with such *positive* feelings. Like old friends met at a party, acquaintance is suddenly renewed with... *Excitement!* Yes, that's it! And... No... no, wait a minute... I'll get it... What's your name now? *JOY!* That's right! And hiding behind her: *Fun!* Where did you come from? Haven't seen you for ages! Now who's that over there? I know you from a long time ago. That soft, shy feeling at the back there. Who is it? Could it be... ? No, it isn't, is it? Yes it is! I didn't recognise you at first, but it is... *Love*... isn't it? Long time, no see.

The baggage

I don't know why I thought that falling in love was a teenager thing. I suppose it was because it had last happened to me when I *was* a teenager. However what I have discovered is that the feelings can strike at any age, and they are the same at any age. I finally understood that when my friend told me about her grandma. She had come into the sitting room to find her grandma (86) sitting next to her gentleman friend (92) on the settee, having a cushion fight! Later Grandma confided, "It's just like being a teenager again!" They married, of course. I should think so too!

So I finally came to see that it was possible to have teenager feelings at any age, but along with them came problems. The biggest problem I found with rediscovering feelings for people of the opposite sex is that feelings of love or attraction for someone had become associated with, or linked to, feelings of agony. You feel the "I love him!" but dread to pursue that feeling because as it re-emerges from the depths you see the cord that so firmly connects it to "He despises me!", which is a feeling you *don't* want pulled out of the depths. To my horror I found that all these positive feelings seemed to be handcuffed to a negative: "I want him – He doesn't want me." "I would like to get to know him – He won't want to know me." "I've lost my heart to him – He will now reject and crush me." "I want to say hello – He wants to say goodbye." "I would like to pursue this connection – He would like to sever all connection."

These reactions weren't based on anything he had

said or done. They weren't based on any response I may or may not have had from him. They just came automatically linked to the feeling in me. How does one break these ties? Some of them seem forged in iron! It seems especially difficult if you are *both* feeling the same way, and yet what man or woman in their 30s, 40s, 50s has come through life emotionally unscathed? There seemed no answer to it. The easiest way to deal with the feelings and their terrifying links was of course to deny they were happening. It doesn't take much to push them down and pretend they're not there. This doesn't help in the long run. They wage guerrilla warfare on you, emerging from the depths of your subconscious in strange and unexpected ways, like not being able to speak when he's in the room.

It was at this point I think that God began to do some serious work on my inner feelings to break some of these links. Part of it was just acknowledging that they were there. When I had strange reactions I would begin to ask myself, "Why?" In this case "Why?" is a good question, because it begins to identify the problem. Like: "Why was it so difficult for me to go up and speak to him?" and "Why did I run away when I saw him approaching?" After all, he was the only one in the room that I wanted to speak to! Slowly it dawned on me that the answer to these "whys" was "Because I was afraid", which led to another question: "What was I afraid of?" The answer was of course that I was afraid of rejection. So, the next time we were in the same room, I just concentrated on not running away (to the loo, to see an acquaintance on the other side of the room, to look at the garden...) and then when he came over I realised that he did want to speak to me and that link "I want to speak to him – he won't want to speak to me" was weakened. It was a strange process. It was like being a teenager again but in a different way; I was unsure of myself, especially in male company, especially when I was attracted to the lovely man in question.

I've already talked about the many and varied ways that God used to heal me. Talking to someone about it helped. Writing about it helped, because it got it all out in the open where it could be seen. The genuine, no-strings-attached compliments of my brothers in the church helped. I taught myself to accept them, to say "Thank you" graciously. Those compliments about my appearance or my characteristics were healing. I suppose that every time I accepted a compliment it was another blow in the battle against the false ideas formed in my head. The friendships of my friends, both male and female, helped. So as I steeled myself to "act normally" with other men, slowly I began to realise that I was acceptable. People, even male people, did enjoy my company and slowly the feelings of rejection receded. It is a process, though.

The most healing thing that I've found is to get into the presence of God. I've a small card on my wall that someone once gave me with a saying of Mother Basilea's: "Seek the presence of Jesus. Through him everything will be solved which you yourself cannot solve." It's been good advice. In the presence of God, everything else falls into perspective. In particular, he seems very good at sorting out emotions. After all, who else knows or understands what is going on inside you? We don't even ourselves understand all the strange reactions we're having. He does, though.

How you find the presence of God depends on who you are and what your life circumstances are. You and God alone in the privacy of your room is good, but so is getting right away. If time and finances permit, or even if they don't, schedule a day, a weekend, a week, or a month away. A quiet day, a retreat, a creative arts weekend, a zappy conference: if it brings you close to God, go there and go again. Go for a walk, put on some worship music, lie in bed at night and think of him; just take whatever moment you have to be with him. You don't have to be anything special; you don't even have to be awake (he can speak through your dreams), and you certainly don't have to *do* anything. Simply being with God is in itself healing. You cannot be in the presence of God and come away the same.

Part of the healing is realising that if the person you admire doesn't want to be involved with you it's not because you are unlovable. As my friend Joanne said to me, "You don't have to marry the first person you fall in love with!" Like a teenager, my fresh, renewed feelings sometimes got carried away too far too fast in speculation and imaginings. I'm finding that I'm having to take to heart myself all the wise advice that I've been dishing out to my own teenagers for years.

But just when my emotions were healed enough to start to think that I might be able to love a man again, I hit another question:

Are divorced Christians allowed to marry again?

God hates divorce (Malachi 2:16). So do I; it causes far too much pain. However, God doesn't hate divorced people. God hates divorce, and so do I: it pulls families apart and rips holes in the fabric of society. But so do arrogance, abuse, abandonment, alcoholism and adultery. God hates those things as well. God hates divorce, but he knows it happens, and he has provided guidelines for us to help us deal with it and minimise its effects.

I hadn't had much teaching on the biblical attitude to divorce. Suddenly I found myself in the unforeseen position of facing a possible divorce, and I didn't dare look at what the Bible had to say about it. I suppose that when you are happily married you don't have to think about the biblical teaching on divorce. And I think I was still wrapped in the vague myths that circulate in the Christian world about divorce. Like many people, I thought God was against all divorce in all circumstances. I was told early on by a high-ranking member of the Church of England that he thought it possible to justify divorce biblically, but not remarriage. Many people quoted, "What God has joined together, let no man put asunder" (Matthew 19:6) at me, so that as I watched my husband walk away from me I felt not only horrendous pain but overwhelming guilt as well. No, I couldn't face looking into the Bible.

So it was a year after my husband left before I realised that there was anything else written in the New Testament about divorce. This is how it happened. I bought myself a copy of *The Message* (Eugene Peterson's translation of the Bible in contemporary English). I took it home and took it out to read and it literally fell open at page 347 (1 Corinthians 7), where I read this:

> God gives the gift of the single life to some, the gift of the married life to others... And if you are married, stay married. This is the Master's command, not mine. If a wife should leave her husband, she must either remain single or else come back and make things right with him. And a husband has no right to get rid of his wife...

So far this was what I had always been taught, and I felt the familiar tightening in my gut. If you are Christians, stay married, and if there are problems, be reconciled. That is the duty of Christians. But what if your husband or wife won't consider reconciliation? Did that mean I was tied to the rest of my life to someone who wasn't there any more?

Further down the page, though, I read this:

On the other hand, if the unbelieving spouse walks out, you've got to let him or her go. You don't have to hold on desperately. God has called us to make the best of it, as peacefully as we can.

Somehow that seemed to ring true with my situation. For me it was a *fait accompli*. Christian or not, he had gone, and wasn't coming back. That term "Christian" was a problem to me. If I had been married to an unbeliever and he had walked out, the natural legalisation of that act by divorce would have been more easily accepted. But because my husband had always claimed a Christian belief, because we were both Christians, many people quoted, "What God has joined together, let no man put asunder" with the implication that somehow we were not allowed to divorce. Are we really teaching from Scripture that Christians married to unbelievers can start a new life if their husband leaves, but if they are married to professing Christians they may not? This put me in an impossible situation. Did that mean that I was forever bound to a man who didn't want me? Was I now also doomed to a loveless life?

When I talked this over with my pastor, he pointed out that my husband might call himself a Christian, but he wasn't acting like one. That reminded me of the teaching of Jesus in Matthew 7:20: "By their fruit you will know them." An apple tree produces apples. A Christian behaves in a Christian manner. What *is* a "believer"? What *is* a "Christian"? In his teaching Jesus always valued honest, heartfelt belief over a form of words or a religious practice. A person might have the form of a belief without it actually affecting what they do. In that case they don't really believe, do they?

"If the unbeliever leaves, let him do so. A believing man or woman is not bound in such circumstances" (1 Corinthians 7:15, NIV). "Not bound" means just that.

God's word says you are free. Free to stay single or marry again. Your choice.

Maybe I was one of the lucky ones. My husband had committed adultery and so in the eyes of the church I had the "get-out clause". Everyone seemed to think that I had a reason for a divorce because of Jesus' reported words in Matthew 19:9 "... I tell you that anyone who divorces his wife, *except for marital unfaithfulness*, and marries another woman commits adultery." So it seems that, because my husband had committed adultery, I was free to remarry without being accused of adultery myself with my new husband. Good! But what about everyone else? This was brought home to me by an incident one day at work.

If you do get divorced, or indeed live through any sort of life crisis, it is best not to be a religious education teacher before you start. (The problem of evil, Why does God allow people to suffer? Death and bereavement, and marriage-and-divorce-in-six-religions are all on my syllabus.) I didn't have a lot of option in this, which is why I found myself one day teaching an exam class of fifteen-year-olds "The Christian View of Marriage and Divorce". They needed to know about it in great detail for the public examination they were about to take.

A loud discussion suddenly erupted on the back row. A group of kids, with no particular religion or experience of the church, had just discovered what Jesus had to say on marriage and divorce and they were horrified! One vocal girl in particular was jabbing at the page of her textbook and saying, "But, Miss, that's so *harsh!*" I looked at where the stabbing finger was landing. "The words of Jesus," it said, "Mark 10: Anyone who divorces his wife and marries another woman commits adultery against her. And if she divorces her husband and marries another man, she commits adultery." There it was in black and white. Loads of heads were bent over the place and young eyes were looking at me. "Yeah, that's harsh, Miss, that's really harsh! I thought Jesus was meant to be good and kind and loving!"

My heart sank. The Jesus I knew WAS good and kind and loving. This might be the only time these kids ever talked about the words of Jesus. How was I going to explain to them he wasn't really harsh? Inwardly I prayed. (I'd like to *think* I said, "You're not harsh, Jesus, how am I going to explain that to them?" But it was probably something more like, "Help! They're calling you harsh – get yourself out of this one!") My explanation to the kids went something like this:

"We've got to get this into context. Jesus was in the middle of a rabbinical debate here. The religious teachers were only interested in trapping him; they didn't really want an answer. Matthew makes that clear in his version of this story (Matthew 19:3-12). We don't have the full conversation reported here in Mark. This bit was obviously remembered because it was so shocking. The reason it was so shocking was that many men at the time believed that they could divorce their wives whenever they wanted, for whatever reason they liked (Matthew 19:3). In those days they thought that someone who committed adultery was doing something so wrong that they deserved the death penalty (Deuteronomy 22:20-22), yet at the same time a man could fancy the girl down the road, give his wife a certificate of divorce without giving her a reason, and then marry the girl he fancied. They still considered themselves good, decent people who had kept the law of God! Jesus was arguing that, although technically they hadn't done anything illegal, in his opinion what they had done was adultery. Matthew 5:32 clarifies this point of his argument a bit: 'If a man divorces his wife *even though she has not been unfaithful* he is guilty of making her commit adultery, and the man who marries her commits adultery also!' So, far from being harsh towards innocent women, Jesus was rightly criticising a religious society that allowed the mistreatment of women by allowing arbitrary and unilateral divorce that women couldn't appeal against. They justified this by saying that Moses – God's spokesman – commanded it. As usual, Jesus was pointing out the hypocrisy of the religious leaders and showing them where they were missing the point." Phew!

In explaining it to the kids at school, it suddenly became clear to me. Jesus is *not* saying in Mark 10 that remarriage automatically makes someone an adulterer; he is saying that in his society they would have been perceived as such, and in that time that was an extremely serious thing to lay at someone's door without justification. Or, as Frank Retief puts it in chapter six of his excellent book *Divorce*:

> Jesus was speaking against this Old Testament background and was not saying that remarriage is adultery, but rather that the unfair treatment of the wife could lead people to see her and the man who married her as adulterers.

Despite what had been quoted to me out of context, there was no prohibition on my remarrying. The only people Jesus was censuring for remarrying were those who rejected their spouse for trivial, arbitrary reasons, and *they* were the ones he blamed, not their rejected partners.

I have since learned that there was a raging theological debate at the time on the interpretation of Deuteronomy 24:1-4, where it says that a man could divorce his wife if he found "some indecency" in her. In the Mishnah (*Mishnah Gittin 9:10*), which was the Jewish commentary on the Old Testament, it says that Rabbi Hillel argued that "some indecency" meant some fault, however trivial – even burning the dinner. Whereas the followers of Rabbi Shammai said it meant some sexual wrongdoing and therefore only allowed divorce on the grounds of adultery, which had to be proved by two male witnesses and not just alleged. Rabbi Akiba however seems to have taught to the letter of the law, pointing out that the passage only required the man to give her a letter, not to say what reasons he had for his action. In this case, just preferring another woman would have been enough reason for divorce. Quite rightly, Jesus points out that this is just legalised adultery.

I did find one qualification to remarriage in the Bible, though. Paul's instruction in 1 Corinthians 7:39 is to marry a believer.

So, to return to the question at the beginning of the chapter, "Will I ever love again?" If I'm sure that reconciliation with my ex is impossible, and if I've left the past, and if I find now that my emotions are healed enough, and should some Christian man come along who should love me, I see no reason in the Bible why I shouldn't get married. Statistically speaking, 75% of divorced people remarry within five years of their divorce. Loving again and finding that true oneness of body, soul and spirit which God intended between a man and a woman looks like a very real possibility. Hmmmmm... I wonder... *Is there anybody out there?*

Chapter 10

How Do I Do Single?

I can see now that if God brought a man into my life it would be possible to love again and even to have a marriage better than the last. I like that idea. However, at the moment I am happily single. Happily? Single? Do those two words go together?

I don't do single very well

I don't do single very well. I'd never had any practice. I went straight from my father's house to my husband's house. I had four children in quick succession. Being alone was certainly not one of my problems. I did experience loneliness as a young mother at home with the children, but my man came home to me every night, bringing, in himself, company and love and support. I'd never lived alone until he left. When you're living in a busy family, with every moment more than accounted for, you long for some time alone. When you return habitually to an empty house, it's not so much fun. God knows that. "It's not good for man to be alone," he said (Genesis 2:18). It's not good for woman either. I wrote a poem about it once. I don't really write poetry as such, more doggerel, but you can read it if you like.

> I don't do single very well.
> It's a sort of unremitting, living hell.
> A constant reminder of all I've lost,
> An ongoing proof of the terrible cost
> That others always have to pay

On behalf of the one who went astray.
I don't do single very well,
I don't like living in emotional hell.

I let that sink into the page for a while, noting the self-pity and angry complaint, and the stark reality of it, and then a second verse, in similar style, formed in my head. It felt like God's reply.

I told you you'd never be alone
(I'm not talking adverts for the latest phone)
I gave it all up, not counting the cost,
To search for and save the lonely and lost.
I took the pain, and the price I paid
On behalf of all who've sinned and strayed.
I love you, adore you, and that you know well.
I've given you my *life, to save you from hell.*

From that you can tell that I'm not very good at poetry. But it got me thinking. There was an eternal exchange that went on at the cross. God in the form of the man Jesus, gave his life in exchange for our empty, barren lives. Jesus is Life. He came to give us life in all its fullness, a fulfilling life. A *single* fulfilling life? To me the two words seemed contradictory.

Loneliness

Being alone is fine sometimes, but when you get too much of it, it becomes loneliness. Loneliness is the biggest problem I've found in being single. How do you describe loneliness? It's an absence; there's nothing *to* describe. Yet loneliness can be a dead weight inside you making even the simplest things difficult. Here's a description of part of one recent evening.

I came home from work on Friday night very tired as

usual, lay down on the bed and fell into a disturbed sleep, the sounds from outside coming in and out of focus. Abigail called upstairs to say that Dad had come to pick her up and she was leaving. The house suddenly seemed very big and the spaces full of silence.

I got up rather than lie there and listen to it. I checked the post – no post, I checked the e-mail – no e-mail. I checked the phone – no messages. I looked at the sadness; it was a dense black cloud, loose and swirling, filling the internal space that was me. Where had it come from? I had no reason to be sad. Nothing bad had happened to me that day. Work was no harder than usual. Everything was functioning as it should. It wasn't even PMT. He left years ago; surely I was used to *that* by now! He has left, but the space he left is ongoing. The loneliness persists. Surely I was used to it by now, had filled the space with other things? But when other things recede, the underlying pain returns. Loneliness.

Be practical, eat something, you always feel tired and sad if your blood sugar levels are low! It's time to eat! Get yourself a meal! I stood in front of the fridge, examining its contents, praying for inspiration. A meal formed itself in my head, thank you God. Why is it always so hard to make a meal for one? I put on some worship music – that's what they always recommend, those kind friends who live in their busy families. "Put on some worship music, change the atmosphere." The words spoke of acceptance and belonging and love, and the music was heartfelt and melodic and reached with scalpel-sharp precision to my deepest sadness. I began to cry. I took a deep breath; the cry turned to a sighing. How long does this go on for?

The sound of the microwave defrosting the frozen package muffled the music. I ignored the black weight inside me and fought my way through the several days' worth of dirty pans collected around the sink, mechanically scrubbing something to cook my dinner in. (Why are teenagers so allergic to washing up?) Scanning the pots and pans I saw a catalogue of the last few days' meals – Tuesday curry, Wednesday fish, Thursday pasta – each saucepan and trivet lying exactly where I'd left it.

The saucepan of water was boiling ferociously now and I reached into the cupboard for the last of the green beans. The worship leader on the CD was lost in a reverie of worship that suddenly seemed at odds with the reality of my surroundings. He was having a good time, and I wondered vaguely if he had a sweet Christian wife at home who cooked his meals and ran the household and took care of the kids while he went out to do his music ministry... Oh dear.

The "Christian music" idea obviously wasn't working, and the sadness hadn't lifted, so I decided to try prayer. I didn't know what to pray, so as I pottered between microwave and cooker, cooker and fridge, fridge and sink, putting together the rest of my meal, I prattled away aimlessly until I found myself leaning against the kitchen door frame, crying from somewhere very deep inside and saying, "Why?". "Why do I have to pray just to get through a 'normal' evening – just to get myself a meal?" "Why is it such a *fight* just to feel normal, just to know some sort of contentment?" The moment passed – they always do – and I made up a tray, dished up my meal and ate it in front of the television.

Rebuilding

Yet there are ways of combating loneliness. Together with God I've been rebuilding my life and I've been learning how to do single, but like all rebuilding it's hard work and it begins by clearing out the old.

Throw out the old

I expect you've had that feeling of wandering through the shattered pieces of your life turning the pieces over and wondering which to keep. The old has gone; the new has come. God kept saying that to me. It took me a long while to realise the extent of that. Slowly, because I couldn't take too much loss at once, I began to throw out what I didn't want in my new life.

Looking back, it started almost immediately. My eldest son helped there. It was in the first week; it was so weird sitting down to a table of three instead of six. I made the spaghetti Bolognese automatically, stirring the meat and tomato mixture, sploshing the red wine into the sauce. As I dished it up there was far too much; I was always making far too much food; that'd be another batch for the freezer then. The boys had set the table. I plonked the bottle down in the middle and as I sat down to eat I poured myself a glass.

Richard's reaction was immediate. "You don't need that!" he said, taking my glass away and removing the bottle. He was only sixteen at the time. I gave him the "Don't usurp the authority of your mother!" speech and reclaimed my glass. But I knew he was right, and I was impressed with his stand. I had poured the wine out of habit. With my husband, I had fallen into the habit of drinking wine with the meal on a daily basis. I didn't have to do that any more, if I didn't want to. It was a strange thought. So much had changed that was totally out of my control and not my choice. Changes that I struggled with and raged over, but slowly I realised I could make changes of my own. Alcohol ceased to become a regular part of my evening meal. (Red wine does add something to a Bolognese sauce, though.)

Spread the load

The gap left by a life partner in your life is huge. There are so many things that they used to do: car mechanics, cooking, finances, whatever. I suppose an instinctive reaction is a longing to find another person to replace the one you lost. But that wouldn't work anyway, because no one is the same as the one you lost, and the two of you lived together in a different way from any other two. So a frantic search for a new partner really is not the answer.

There are other ways of filling the gaps. You have to find new ways of doing these things. This doesn't happen all at once, but slowly you find ways of spreading the load. Don't be afraid to ask for help, as people are usually glad to be able to DO something for you. The hardest thing for other people is to see that you are hurting and not to be able to do anything about it.

I felt such a fool for not knowing anything about a car's engine or what to do with it. Eventually I got up the courage to ask a colleague at school if he could explain it to me. "No idea," he said. "I don't know a thing about engines. I always take my car to the garage and they fix it."

That in itself was a revelation to me. Not all men fix cars! It was OK to say "I don't know" and take it to the garage! In the same way, not all women like ironing, and most I know are not *cordon bleu* cooks. But I asked *another* colleague the questions I had about car engines and he was delighted to help. He didn't mind explaining at all and I sensed the relief he felt that he could actually *do* something.

The key is to spread the load. Don't keep asking the same people. Many of the things my husband used to deal with, such as the bills and finances, I've learnt to do myself, and in the process I've gained a new sense of independence and satisfaction. Other things, such as fixing the car, I can pay a mechanic to do. I thought those huge spaces that he left in my life when he went would never get filled, but by and large they have been.

Forward planning

Being single is hard work. I haven't found a way round that. Many of the things that once came automatically, like company, help with the house, holidays, talking through problems, excursions, celebrations and fun, now have to be actively planned in advance. That takes time, effort and emotional energy. It is much, much easier to do things together with someone than on your own. You help each other along. For example, it's just plain easier to move heavy things with someone else around! So things like clearing out the shed or moving the furniture before decorating take less than half the time if you can find someone to help you. This is true for men as well as women. A single friend of mine finally got his loft sorted out when a few days' holiday and a passing friend coincided. The two of them were able to rig up a pulley system and get rid of an old redundant water tank and several decrepit mattresses – an impossible task for one but possible with two.

I'm learning from my single friends. Those of us who have been married may well know what it is to have another person at hand to help, but single people have never had that luxury. I have learnt so much from my long-time single friends. I have learnt that it really does help to plan ahead. Let's face it, Christmas, summer holidays, bank holidays and birthdays are going to be difficult. They are difficult for everyone who has not got a ready-made family to spend them with. It really does help to have something planned in advance rather than let the date just creep up on you. It's my birthday soon and I'm going with a friend to Bath, a beautiful English town, for a walking weekend with a barn dance. We've joined the Christian Ramblers' Club (or Crazy Rambling

Christians, as I prefer to call them) and their weekends and events make little oases of friendship and fun in my life.

Christmas can be very difficult, and people cope with it in different ways. What you plan doesn't matter as long as you have a plan. Some people go to their mum's or their sister's. Some invite friends to them. Others do something completely different, like helping out at a soup kitchen, or taking a holiday abroad in a country where they don't celebrate Christmas!

Establish a new network

There's no longer that one person at home to talk to about the strains of the day, or a specific problem you have to deal with, but now I do have friends near and far whom I can talk to on the phone. Some are good in an emotional crisis; some know the answers to practical problems; some empathise with the particular problems of my work, and others just like to chat! You soon learn. The trick is not to overload any one person.

What I've been doing, I now realise, is establishing a new network of friends and contacts for this new life. I was astounded, and yet somehow relieved, to find out that most people lose 80% of their network of friends after a divorce. I was astounded because that figure is so high. I was relieved because it had happened to me, and I had thought that it was just because I was a particularly unlikeable person. It takes time to establish a new network, and I don't think there is any way around that. It just does take time to make new friends and re-establish contacts with old ones. It takes effort, too, and it seems so unfair that you have to do this. That's because it *is* unfair. There are advantages, though. My life is very different now from what it was six years ago, yet I have to say it's more the way I want it. I have an independence now that

I never had before, and a sense of fulfilment I never had either.

If this all seems too much at the moment and you'd be happy just to cope with the problems of today, then give yourself a break and leave all this for another day. But if there are decisions that have to be made, then you might want to ask yourself the question, "What do I want?" Now may be the time to think about doing what you've always wanted to do. Get that qualification, change your job, start your own business, spend time on your art, music or writing, get involved with that crazy church, volunteer for that charity you support, decorate your home in the colours you like, save up for that trip abroad, go on your first ever retreat... Whatever! The answers to the question "What do I want in my new life?" will be as varied as the people asking it. If you are at that stage but don't quite know how to go about it, the book *Where Do I Go From Here?* by Dr Kenneth Ruge was recommended to me, and is very helpful.

God as Husband?

Women had said to me in the past that losing their husband was like losing a limb. I was shocked then, but now I find it too mild a simile. I felt as if I had been completely ripped in two. One whole side of me was raw and bleeding. God immediately stepped to my side to cover that wound and fill the gap. I had lost a husband and gained a Husband. Many of us have learned to relate to God as Father, but Husband is a biblical image too.

Isaiah 54:5 reads, "For your Maker is your Husband – the Lord of Hosts is his name – the Holy One of Israel is your Redeemer; he is called the God of the whole earth."

When I first read this, the bit in parentheses struck me – the Lord of HOSTS (of spiritual beings) is his name! THE GOD OF THE WHOLE WORLD! Wants to be your husband! That's amazing! Yet there I was, bemoaning the fact that I'd been left. An invisible husband wasn't what I wanted. I wanted the old one to be there. On the other hand it is a far worse desolation to be without God, or at least to feel that you are without God, than to be without a husband. I'd lost my husband but I was so grateful that I hadn't lost my God! On the same day Ezekiel 16:60 also came up in my readings: "I will keep the pledge I made with you when you were young. I will establish an everlasting covenant with you forever." Here God is promising me what my ex-husband couldn't. My husband broke the pledge he made when we were very young but the pledge GOD made will never be broken. It seemed that God wanted me to take this "God-as-Husband" idea seriously. So I did. I took him very seriously, almost vehemently, at his word on this one.

It was the practical things that really got to me. The DIY and the bills and the household emergencies.

"If you are going to be Husband to me, you need to deal with everything he dealt with!"

"Yes."

"I mean in practical reality!"

"Yes."

"Because I don't know how to do these things!"

"There's never any need to worry."

I knew what *that* meant. It was our code for Philippians 4:6, which had always been a key verse for me. I like the way *The Message* puts it:

> Don't fret or worry. Instead of worrying, pray. Let petitions and praises shape your worries into prayers, letting God know your concerns. Before you know it, a sense of God's wholeness, everything coming together for good, will come and settle you down. It's wonderful what happens when Christ displaces worry at the center of your life.

So instead of turning to my husband for this type of daily support, I turned to my God who said one of his names was Husband. Now the problem phrase in the quote above is that "instead of". As I've said, I've had plenty of practice with this verse over the 30 odd years I've been a Christian, but I haven't quite managed the "instead of". I am making progress, though, and I can now confidently say that I've got as far as "as well as". So that's how I dealt with it. *As well as* worrying, I prayed. I certainly got good at letting God know my concerns.

Do you know something? He sorts it. As that French lady said to me the week I learned my husband was leaving, "God takes care of everything." How? I hear some of you saying. In many and varied ways, is all I can say to that. Obviously God isn't a physical being; he's a spiritual being. You can't see him, hear him or touch him, although you can sense his presence sometimes. (How do we do that? Is it a sort of sixth sense?) So he didn't manifest in my living room bearing a hammer to fix the problem. Nor did the problem miraculously fix itself when I prayed about it.

However, a solution always presented itself. Sometimes I found the right advice and the strength to do it myself (the bathroom tiles are still looking good), sometimes other people were happy to help (I'd never have got my sitting room decorated without Trevor, Joanne and Mark – thanks guys!). More often than not a "chance" conversation would throw up an excellent workman with time to spare (fantastic job on the door handles and roof, Pete), and if that hasn't convinced you, get this: when the boiler went wrong I looked up plumbers in *Yellow Pages* and prayed about which one to phone. Not only was he in, but he was able to come out that day *and* he subsequently proved to be honest and reasonably priced. Now tell me that's not a miracle!

"But just a cotton-picking minute," I can hear you

saying. "If God is such a husband to you and if everything is so fine and hunky-dory, what was with that bit on loneliness at the beginning of the chapter? What's more, how come you were so overcome with loneliness on Friday last week that you cried on the phone for an hour to a friend and spent Saturday writing 2,500 words about it? Huh?" (How did you know about that? It was too long to put in the book!)

Good point. And one I've pondered on long and hard. There are times when I am alone here and it's fine. There are times too when the felt presence of God keeps me company – but you can't presume on that. Nevertheless there have also been many times when the ongoing loneliness has been very hard indeed. Doing everything by yourself is wearying and isolating and very lonely. That's when I end up going to the supermarket just to talk to the checkout girls. Or I coo at a passing baby in its pram, because at least I usually get a response from them. So many people say to me, "Well at least you've got God," as I go home to yet another lonely evening, that I begin to feel guilty for being lonely. I *have* got God; he is wonderful, I couldn't live without him, yet I am still lonely. In the end I decided to ask God about it.

"It's not good for man to be alone," he said.

"Yes, I know," I said. "Nor woman either, that's my point."

"When did I say that?"

"What?"

"When did I say that?"

"Genesis... to Adam... Garden of Eden... it's obvious."

"When, though."

Does he do this to you too? Give you a question and then just leave you to work it out? Infuriating, isn't it? What did he mean, "when"? We know when! It was nearly at the beginning, when the world had been made, when Adam had been created, when he was living in paradise with the plants and animals, that's when!... Then I got it! I felt such an idiot I had to say "red" backwards!

He was in the Garden of Eden, in PARADISE, with everything he needed, before the Fall, when he was still in full, constant, walking, talking, fellowship with GOD. That's when! And even THEN God himself says, "It is not good for man to be alone."

"When he was in full fellowship with you! You said it when he was in full fellowship with you!" What a relief. You see, God is God. We call him "HE", which makes him sound like a human being, but in fact he's a spiritual being. Human beings need God. They also need other human beings. God himself says so. So don't feel bad if you feel lonely. It's a normal human reaction to being by yourself. We weren't made to live alone, without human company. The answer is to rebuild a network of friends and family and contacts to fill some of those lonely times. God will help you with this. He knows it's not good for you to be alone too much. It takes time, but it will happen.

Restoration

The only way I know how to do this new life is by starting from the premise that it's all been handed over to God. Once that is done then the amazing creative power of the almighty and all-loving King of the Universe is unleashed in your life, so watch out! Anything could happen! Remember *Stingray*? *"Stingray! Stingray! Diddle urdle urdle. Anything could happen in the next half-hour!"* (I do apologise to anyone under the age of 45 for whom that last outburst may be totally meaningless.) Forget *Stingray*! This is GOD we're talking about. Anything really *could* happen, anything you want, anything he wants for you. Dream the Impossible Dream and then watch it come true! He will do it because he loves you.

My problem is that I don't believe that God wants to

give me the good things he does. He's rebuilding in precious gems, while I expect breeze block. It's trying to get my head around the fact that he thinks I am worth so much. He promises life in all its fullness, but somehow I still expect dreariness. Is it possible that a single life could be fulfilling? Is it possible that he might have planned a new marriage for me? Is it possible that his plans for my life might involve some unknown scheme or project that is even better than I could imagine? I'm beginning to believe it might be true. Single or not, my future will be very good, and it is already expanding in ways I could never have imagined. Yes! He's building in precious gems.

We all know that saying of Paul's, "All things work together for good, for those who know God and are called according to his purpose" (Romans 8:28). When I look at the bigger picture in my life I have to say that it's true. The process of rebuilding does take time and the foundations take longest, but rebuild a fulfilling life for you, he will. He cannot do less, because he loves you. He only heals us as slowly as he does to give us a chance to get used to the changes. It would all be a bit too much if we had all the operations in the same week. Sometimes it feels as if the process will never end, or as if the job of restoration is impossible. That's because it *is* impossible – for us; but God's kindness is extreme; his love is overwhelming and his power to heal is infinite. He really cannot fail to bring you life because he is in you and he IS Life.

Right from the beginning God was already talking to me about rebuilding. Like a city destroyed after a war, much is lost when your married life is destroyed, but it does give you the opportunity to decide how you want to rebuild. You can choose to build in the old style, like some of the painstakingly restored towns in Germany, where medieval and Renaissance techniques and materials were rediscovered so as to build in authentic style. Or you can choose an entirely new, state-of-the-art building on the same site. Or something in-between and very creative. I once saw a restored cathedral in France where the architect had kept what remained of the three walls still standing after the bombing but replaced the fourth with concrete and glass. It was stunning.

The question is, "What do you want?" It's a difficult question, I know, and in some ways it's a frightening one, but it does allow for new and exciting opportunities, and don't forget that the chief architect on this site is God himself. He's a real expert on restoration and his building styles are innovative, top-quality and creative in the extreme. In those early days of confusion it was hard to believe that a restored life was possible; come on, it was hard to believe that *normality* would ever be possible again, but in God all things really are possible.

As I write I can honestly say that my life now is more fulfilling than it has ever been. I'm in leadership in my church at a very exciting time in its development. I have the privilege of being allowed to preach. My children love me and are growing up into fine young adults, maybe a little wiser than they might otherwise have been. I am very proud of them. I have strong connections with people on the other side of the world, in Kenya. I am writing this book! I have a successful, if stressful, career in teaching. Life is good. I have emerged from that storm into the sunshine again. God is good and the process of learning how to live a happy, fulfilled single life goes on.

Postscript

"Don't be wishing you were someplace else or with someone else. Where you are right now is God's place for you. Live and obey and love and believe right there. *God, not your marital status, defines your life*" (1 Corinthians 7:17, *The Message*).

In preparing for this second edition of *Missing Being Mrs* (first published in 2004) I re-read all the letters I'd received (yes even ten years ago we used to write to each other on paper) and all the Amazon reviews. Then I started to cry. It is a very long time since the days when tears came so easily that I habitually carried tissues everywhere, but these tears were not tears of sadness. I was simply deeply moved that the book had helped so many other people, men and women, who were going through something similar. God bless you all.

A lot of you asked "What happened next?". Well, I spent ten happy years as a single person bringing up my children, working full time as a teacher, contributing to my local church and pursuing my own interests in whatever spare time and holidays I had. I travelled, visiting Africa and Australia (lifetime ambitions) and Crete and Malta (fantastic archaeology). I developed my tiny garden into a haven of flowers. I did far too much knitting when it suddenly came back into fashion. Oh, and I wrote a couple of books. I surprised myself, because there was a time when I thought that none of those things would ever be possible again. The biggest surprise to me in those ten years was that the original arrangements made for the children changed over time. I presumed when the family first broke up that I would never live in the same house as my daughters again, but as they got older and more independent, they both chose, at different times, to make their main home base with me again. My sons spent some years with their father too. So we were all able to have that day to day closeness with all the children again. My life has certainly been a lot happier than I could ever have imagined in my darkest days.

After ten years of single life I met, and eventually married, a man who himself had been through a difficult divorce. It took a long while for our friendship to develop into something more permanent as we both had trust issues that we had to work through. After all I was wary of the 50 per cent of people who are male and he was more than happy to avoid the 50 per cent of the world that was female! Our current relationship is a huge delight to us both and feels like an amazing gift from God.

After this book was written many people commented that I had left out the children's issues and how I coped with the difficulties the family break up had made for *them*. Well that's right. *Missing Being Mrs* tells *my* story and covers how I dealt with the emotional side of being involved in a relationship break up. However, in 2013 I wrote a very different book *The Essential Guide to Children and Separation*, published by Lion Hudson. This is a practical guide for anyone interested in how to help the children who are involved in a family break up whether parent, grandparent, family friend, pastor or teacher. It includes all I learned from dealing with my own children as well as *their* insights and helpful comments from many other children who have been through the experience. It describes how family break up affects children differently at various ages and has advice on step-parenting as well. It also has lots of suggestions and tips on loving, communicating and parenting at a distance. As it says on the back cover "... divorce may mean the end of a marriage, but does not need to be the end of the world for the children involved." It certainly wasn't the end of the world for my own children who are now all grown up, with long-term partners of their own.

I've just turned sixty, I don't look a day over fabulous (if I believe my birthday cards) and I have two grandchildren who are skilled at making me laugh. I've left teaching and retired to the country and I'm looking forward to what this next stage of my life will bring.

Bibliography

Divorce, Frank Retief, Struik Christian Books

Suddenly Single, Phil Stanton, Kingsway

All Alone?, Jill Worth & Christine Tufnell, Paternoster

Where Do I Go from Here?, Dr Kenneth C Ruge, McGraw-Hill

The Message, Eugene Peterson, NavPress

The Transformation of the Inner Man, John and Paula Sandford, Victory House